RE-BUILDING on ROCK

...Leaders re-creating Culture

Doug Booker

Co-authored by:

Mark Broadway &

Derek Kenner, Ph.D.

Original Copyright 2010

Revised & Republished 2014

All rights reserved.

ISBN-13: 978-1495983634

ISBN-10: 1495983633

(Available on KINDLE)

Kansas City

913.232.0244

www.bookertraining.com

Published by
Drambert Publishing Company

Table of Contents

Introductory Thoughts & Purpose	p 5
An Analogy – Turtle & the Hare	p 11
Part I: Conversation (The Solution)	p 18
A Framework	p 23
Implementing Keys	p 44
What won't work	p 46
Part II: Story: REBUILDING on ROCK	p 49
CLO Talk to Mgrs	p 52
CEO Wrap-up	p 103
Part III: Apply to YOUR WORLD	p 113

(Mid-level manager, small business owner, superintendent/principle, church pastor, Community leader/mayor, Independent office/staff manager)

A Final Note / Conclusion	p 121
Author / Co-authors	p 122
Appendices	p 128

> *"Dedicated to those who helped me learn about Leadership, Workplace Culture & People!"*

- ❖ Clients, associates and friends with whom I have learned

- ❖ To those who are open to learn and improve their leadership

- ❖ To those who are led, that they may understand and become leaders

- ❖ My family who taught me much; my parents who are great leaders

- ❖ Ron Black, who led me to the Lord; Sydney, my wife who has led me closer

- ❖ The U.S. Army and military leadership examples and experiences

- ❖ Kansas State University ROTC cadets who allowed me to teach them

- ❖ My two great kids who suffered and survived my learning of leadership (in parenting)

Some Introductory Thoughts & Purpose

"Any organization functioning <u>without</u> ...trained, developed Leadership & Productive, positive Relationships... Is performing at only a fraction of its actual potential. And that's most organizations!"

I hope you will find this book to be hugely beneficial in numerous ways. Two goals are clearly intended: 1) that it be applicable to *your* world and 2) that it will be an individual and organizational resource for growing leaders, individuals, teams and organizations. My work here is about the *learning process*. First creating an awareness of need (motivation), telling a story, and then plenty of practical application. Because of the importance of 'repetition' in changing habits/behaviors, there is a certain amount (of repetition of ideas & concepts) worked in here for sure. Lastly to help you digest and internalize your thinking as you read, I have provided lots of space for you to take notes. This book will hopefully be forever, a valuable resource for you the reader. If I am successful, you will practice the concepts and change behaviors (yours and those of others). The book is applicable to leadership teaching in the workplace, within communities, business settings, church, school, supervision, teaching, coaching and even parenting - virtually anywhere that requires LEADERSHIP.

The ASSUMPTIONS that were presented in our first book, Teaching Fishing, are totally connected to this book. It is not critical that you review those assumptions; however it might be a good idea! To view the first book or just to review the assumptions, contact me through website or email me for a copy of them, doug@bookertraining.com.

"*Managers* MAINTAIN;

While Leaders

IMPROVE, GROW & MAKE BETTER!"

A 'small' percentage of corporations, companies and organizations of all types are facing the reality that talk must become action regarding our most valuable resource – people. Real behavioral leadership-change had better happen sooner rather than later, in order to survive in our ever-increasing competitive global environment. The workforce, facilitated by effective leadership, must become perceptive, flexible, collaborative-thinking and 'ahead of the game' regarding change (for all industries). More and more, organizational leadership teams (and not just some short-lived consulting effort) need to understand concepts such as Org. Development, Change

Facilitation, Culture-improving, and Individual & Org. Behavior; and for sure to begin practicing REAL LEADERSHIP!

Only through a commitment by leadership from the top, carrying down through subordinate leaders and leadership, can real change sustain itself. This is especially true when speaking of changing people and behavior! Organizations will have to commit resources to develop a different definition of 'what leadership means' and to see it become the new reality. Consider the challenges we already have *when we are all working together locally*, and then picture the leadership, teamwork, relationships & communicating challenges *as we attempt them* VIRTUALLY and GLOBALLY...yikes! We must identify the kind of culture that is desired...and then lay out plans to get there. Finally we must understand and become true critical-thinkers regarding how to make *people our most valuable resource.* Posters on the walls of HR or PR briefings (about this slogan) don't make it real and just don't cut it any longer!

It takes a big-picture, long-term approach to address these factors, and a discontinuation of 'programs-of-the-month, fads or jumping on the bandwagon of the latest Quality or Business initiative. LEADERSHIP is *stuff* that has been talked (seminars/retreats held and books written) about for many years, and then forgotten or disbanded when it comes to making it happen. More often than not, <u>the talk fails to become reality when leaders realize that this is about their own personal leadership behaviors</u>. This hits too close to home for some, there are ego issues and/or there is just no time for this leadership *stuff*. Schedules are too full already - doing management *stuff*!?! There is no mistake about it, the winners of tomorrow are those organizations that see *this*, understand *it*, and facilitate making it their new reality! *'This & it'* = LEADERSHIP. Individual leaders and organizational leadership must be willing to personally change and commit to implementing a sustainable leadership & people-development process.

> 📖   Once again, this book and its message are not about one-shot seminars and retreats; costly canned programs; a couple of months of meetings; rah-rah speeches or any other short-lived initiative!

It *is* about that worn out phrase, <u>walking vs. talking</u> when it comes to leading folks; becoming the *Best of the Best* in our worlds.

"When Leadership changes,

Teams / Organizations change;

...Leaders must go first."

(A Zig Ziglar special, I believe)

Concepts, terminology and topics addressed within:

- 📖 **Building a Culture**
- 📖 **Servant Leadership**
- 📖 **Teaching and Facilitating**
- 📖 **People-systems**
- 📖 **Human Capital**
- 📖 **Chain of Command understanding**
- 📖 **Growing people**
- 📖 **Succession Planning**
- 📖 **Personal Mastery**
- 📖 **Buy-in and Consensus building**
- 📖 **Mentoring**
- 📖 **Organizational Development and Behavior**
- 📖 **Team Development (TEAMership)**
- 📖 **Critical Thinking**
- 📖 **Relationship & Communications**

Note: Before continuing on, you may want to take a quick peek at Part III, on page 147. There I have provided a brief discussion related to the application of this book's messages to 'other worlds'. Not just the large workplaces - but within communities, small businesses, for individual managers, independent offices, churches, etc.

> *"Therefore everyone who hears these*
> *Words of mine and puts them into practice*
> *Is like a wise man*
> *Who built his House on the Rock?"*
> Matthew 7:24(NI)

The implication, connection and *fact* here is that if an organization addresses LEADERSHIP, RELATIONSHIPS and TEAMERSHIP effectively, the organization will be one with a solid foundation. Adding in faith, God and His Word further solidifies things for sure. This book's conversation and story discusses a scenario and approach for beginning a new culture - addressing LEADERSHIP and LEADERS first. Part I goes into some detail about a process of instituting real leadership qualities, traits, skills and behaviors into any organization. Part II is a story about an organization (Tool Box Inc and its CLO, Booker). Senior Management is gathering the entire company's management & supervision team for a day of getting the WORD out. It is 'visioning' about a new organizational leadership culture, blue skies, hope, and commitment - and how (TBI) is going to go about making it happen. This is *day one of a new beginning* of a never-ending process (and not just another program this time). We all have 'been there, done that' with short-lived programs, huh?

AN ANALOGY

"The Turtle, not the Hare
Won in the long run...
...because it is a long run!"

Organizations that attempt to develop leadership and teamwork (fix morale, attempt to make people happy, repair negativity, do change-recovery, fend off union efforts, address turnover, etc), typically approach it as a program or event! These attempts might be compared to how the Hare approached 'the race' in the fable of the HARE and the TORTOISE.

Just as the Hare *did*, so organizations *do* in attempting to deal with Leadership, Culture, Teamwork, Turnover, People development, etc. They sprint around from this point (or) program (or) idea (or) fad to another; trying one thing after another. This is in lieu of understanding the root cause and actually solving the problem. They leap from program to program, or try gimmicks, giveaways, promise things and/or temporary training fixes. Truly you may want to ponder this right now for a moment. Think of your organization (or past organizations). How is improving LEADERSHIP, RELATIONSHIPS and TEAMERSHIP dealt with...if it is at all?

> 📖 What attempts have been made.......what programs have been tried or are you suffering through right now...how many quick fixes haven't worked?

Getting back to our race between the Tortoise and the Hare; in case you are not familiar with it - the Tortoise (turtle) won the race. Let me share the actual story here, paraphrased and adapted from a number of different sources online....

Once upon a time there was a rabbit (hare) always bragging about how he was faster than anyone? He had for a long time teased the turtle (tortoise), again boasting of his speed and the turtle's lack of!

Getting ever so tired of the rabbit, the turtle one day responded with: "Undoubtedly you are fast Mr. Hare, but not unbeatable for sure!" The rabbit laughed in the turtle's face, rolling around chuckling at the bizarre thought, at least to him.

"Who could possibly beat me in a race? Surely not you. For that matter I doubt there's anyone who could. But how about you Mr. Tortoise, you want to race me?"

The turtle clearly frustrated with the rabbit's continued bragging, accepted the challenge, "Of course I will, let's do it tomorrow!"

They agreed on the course layout, the race was planned and at dawn the following morning, they were at the starting line. READY-SET-GO... The rabbit 'chilled out, even yawning and sleepily watched' as the turtle began to meander down the race course. "Hey Mr. Tortoise, take your time, as if you have a choice," he chuckled as he hollered, "I will take a short nap and catch up to you shortly."

The rabbit awoke after a bit and looked around for the turtle. He spied him just a short distance down the course, having only made it maybe a third of the way. The rabbit sprinted quickly toward the turtle, and then was distracted, thinking he might just as well have some breakfast before going on. He hopped around eating some carrots, cabbage and other leafy favorites. The hot sun and heavy meal made him tired and he fell asleep again.

A quick glance down the trail saw the turtle was still only halfway and after a quick dash to get ahead of him, the Hare decided on some more shut-eye. He obviously could just dash past the turtle and easily win in a bit. He fell asleep with a smile on his face, envisioning the big finish and the potential disappointment of the turtle as he cruised by to the finish line.

The turtle plodded forward methodically and steadily, not losing focus or stopping for anything. He had one goal and was determined as he plodded along.

The rabbit woke up and peeked out from his tired eyelids to see how far along the turtle was down the course. He realized the turtle was only yards from the finish! The turtle was close, but with a hard push, the rabbit figured he could still win. He hopped and leaped as hard as he could, gasping and breathing heavily.

The rabbit began to panic realizing the race was going to be close. He was so close, but his last jump, hop and dash were just a little too late as the turtle moseyed across the finish line. Mr. Tortoise had won. The rabbit's over-confidence, lack of focus, distractions, ego and lack of concern had cost him the race.

Beaten, exhausted and disgraced he laid flat on the ground by the turtle, seeing the big smile on Mr. Tortoise's face.

"Mr. Rabbit, the race does not always go to the fastest, but to the one who just keeps on going!" the turtle said with a smirk.

> 📖 Before we continue on, what's the story have to do with your organization's past or maybe even current approaches to Leadership, People development, Teamwork, Workforce satisfaction, Turnover, etc?

Let's break the story down a bit, and do some comparison and analysis:

1) The arrogance and confidence of the rabbit could represent the attitude and mindset that management (and managers) takes regarding leadership. The thinking of how we are BEING LEADERS because we are in charge; we are the smartest/most knowledgeable; we possess best ideas or simply because we have a title.

2) The sprinting and darting around of the rabbit relates to the temporary and/or short-term fixes organizations try when this leadership thing isn't really working. These are attempts like sending managers to seminars, bringing in speakers, surveying the workforce, motivational programs, making promises, suggestion boxes, giving bonuses or other giveaways, etc.

3) Losing the race might be the same as the organization when they never really understand this leadership thing. Organizations, management and all of us in general have become numb to these dynamics. We lose

when we have come to accept ineffective teamwork, management and dysfunctional relationships – as just the way it is, people will be people and there is nothing we can really do about it. *[That's definitely 'losing the race'].*

4) Now how about that turtle? He saw one thing, and focused on it, not allowing anything to get in the way of the goal or objective. He is always moving toward the vision, the root cause and/or end-goal! What we are after is strong, developed LEADERSHIP, RELATIONSHIPS and TEAMERSHIP.

The Tortoise just methodically stayed the course, focused on the vision and eventually won. Meanwhile the Hare just sprinted around trying things, losing focus, trying to be clever, wasting time,...eventually losing. One might even compare the Hare's belief that his speed would overcome anything - as the same thinking that managers will overcome any shortcomings in leadership – simply because they have more technical know-how.

Let's be clear – this (way of thinking about all this) is not some conscious, devious mental process. It is just a subtle unconsciousness that creeps into individual thinking, organizational practices and culture. Isn't it part of your organization's thinking and culture...maybe even your own thinking? I will mention this again, but let me emphasize that <u>none of this discussion is intended to suggest organizations, management and/or managers are bad people</u>. In fact, my belief is that the vast majority of managers are good people. This is about bad management practices and a complete lack of leadership understanding within our society.

To that end, the purpose of this book is to challenge the current thinking of people responsible for developing leadership and essentially organizations as a whole. Oh yeah, we are also intending to challenge YOUR thinking! Not just to challenge the thinking, but also to provide some answers. For those not yet actually in leadership roles, this could and should be a great resource for understanding your bosses and management. It will also prepare you for *your day of leadership* (versus just becoming the next ineffective manager that fell into this trap)! *As I mentioned in our first book, where else do you think you will receive any preparation?

📖 Let's say a *perfect* organizational people-system (great relationships, leadership, etc) is a (10), and a totally dysfunctional one is a (1)... What number would you give your own team, your organization, past teams & organizations?

____ / 10

📖 Now, is that losing? ☺☹

Part I

"Columbus set sail with three ships to discover and begin a new, exciting world. Maybe your organization should set sail toward a new world as well - with

The **LEADER***ship,*
The **TEAMER***ship &*
The **RELATION***ship!"*

THE SOLUTION

ALL organizations (or maybe just 99%☺) suffer from ineffective leadership, mostly due to essentially one flawed assumption. That assumption: everyone somehow gets LEADERSHIP UNDERSTANDING, SKILLS AND BEHAVIORS by just spending time in the organization, gaining expertise and experience in the business, technical and operational *stuff*. [Or maybe because we have an education/degree!]

While our first book covered this dilemma in great depth; this book's focus is providing some thinking regarding HOW TO solve the problem; and providing answers to resolve the dilemma. The question here, whether you are a manager yourself (or for the organization as a whole) is this:

> 📖 How do we develop real leaders and sustain real and continued progress in individual and organizational leadership?

One source says this about why it (developing real leadership) is so difficult for an organization:

"...*a lack of clarity of goals, performance criteria and measurable results for the management and managers...*" I concur completely; now ponder this for a moment...

- What competencies or evaluation criteria are measured regarding managers, supervisors and/or leaders anywhere?

- *what are your organization's leadership expectations?*

- Do we allow any other employee to not be evaluated based on a set of specific expectations/accountabilities?)

Let me relate some of my beliefs as to why this situation exists - why leadership development is ineffective and unsustainable?

* In the *best of situations*, organizations will pursue Leadership Development by giving management folks 'some' training, (a workshop, seminar, program or maybe some 'extended Leadership Academy concept', etc).

* The individual manager or maybe the HR department might put some focus on traits, qualities and skills needed to supervise people. Possibly they may look at some Personal Leadership *stuff* (time management, organizing, personality profiling, etc); or a focus on self-development.

* Some organizations might even do some short term program involving work-relationships, expensive assessments, surveying the workforce, etc, (doing little with results).

These are typically sporadic activities, discussions or programs at best; certainly they are not well thought out long-term strategies for LEADERSHIP DEVELOPMENT PROCESSES or SYSTEMS. <u>And remember, this is only in the best of situations</u>, the pro-active organization! Many of these efforts consist of substantive 'good stuff' no doubt (since I have facilitated plenty of these types of events or programs for companies☺).

It is not that those efforts are bad. However we have a critical piece left un-addressed; leaving any of these efforts un-sustainable and non-behavior changing.

>>> There must be implementation and creation of a process to define, and begin evaluating and measuring leadership behaviors through a set of Competencies, and accountabilities. <<<

This process must be never-ending, involving all in establishing and defining these; and developing a system whereby leaders are providing routine feedback (coaching & mentoring) of their subordinate leader's development.

> 📖 Does any of this sound familiar? Aside from evaluation of a manager's team/department productivity, how is each individual's leadership evaluated?

A FRAMEWORK
... For real sustainable organizational leadership development!

Again, this process must include the development, identification, upfront agreement and assessment of a set of Leadership Competencies. These are the new expectations and <u>competencies</u> that will be used with all leaders (LEADERSHIP QUALITIES, SKILLS/TRAITS and BEHAVIORS). These are then applied to all leaders from the frontline supervisory role to the execs at the top! They are to be used for hiring, firing, coaching, training, mentoring, evaluation, promotion, bonuses, etc.

To be sure, this is not something to jump into without a significant amount of thought & discussion…and consensus and commitment! There must be buy-in from the top. Trust me, some won't like this. From the top, most VPs, execs, managers and supervisors have been allowed to 'lead' in any way to produce results. Now we are going to start critiquing and evaluating skills and competencies such as LISTENING, RESOLVING CONFLICT, GROWING INDIVIDUALS & TEAMS, JUDGMENT, RELATIONSHIPS, CARING, ETHICS, etc! Some will not like this☺.

The rules are changing from vagueness and a lack of expectations and standardization about management that has been going on, well, forever. There will be struggles, and there will be some management people leave. Some on their own, and some because they do not fit into the mode, model and new culture now sought after – real LEADERSHIP, RELATIONSHIPS and TEAMERSHIP.

Here are some concepts briefly covered; hopefully detailed enough to allow for understanding of the intent. If not, give me a call, sincerely! These are strategies, ideas and concepts I have accumulated, adopted, learned and developed over the last couple of decades. For sure, this framework is from the ideas, approaches, thinking and learning of others I have associated with, and presented to you here as my thinking. These are practices and principles learned and utilized in working with organizations, personal coaching, teamership efforts and overall culture development. Although it is shared here and laid out for an organization of some size, the concepts are applicable (if you do some thinking) to any LEADER and his/her TEAM.

So let's get started. Here are the pieces that are involved with any REBUILDING on ROCK effort.

...A Dozen to consider / Steps to Success!

1. **The Organizational Leader (OL)**...The OL's Executive Leadership/Management Team ELMT)...

2. **Visioning Acceptance** with all, each level...

3. **Establishment of Leadership Competencies**...

4. **Supervisor Team / Frontline Leaders** (FLL)...

5. The entire **Leadership Team / 'Chain of Command'**...

The following pieces are a part of discussions and development of the team of leaders at each level beginning with the top and moving downward.

6. **Historical understanding**....impacts and baggage

7. **Communication** Systems, Procedures and Processes

8. **Organizational Trust and Relationships**

9. Our **Leadership Practices /Principles**

10. **Problem-solving & Decision-making**

11. **Learning and Idea-handling**

12. **Change Implementation** Understanding, Skills & Strategies

---

SUCCESSION PLANNING (An absolute imperative to real sustainment. Must be part of this. To be discussed in future books)

This is not intended to be a precise and exact 'must' sequence. The exact approach that you follow must be determined by the organization's leadership, together. As the process evolves and develops, we must model what we are trying to achieve!?! As we begin the creation of our LEADERSHIP COMPETENCIES for the organization and all leaders, this is done with the *involvement* of leaders from the top to bottom. Up and down, down and up... This is done until we are on the same page and have achieved consensus on the best set of Leadership Competencies for the organization.

NOTE: I have shared a set of competencies in this book that are purely intended to be an example. No doubt good stuff (since I came up with them☺), but yours are not for me to determine. All of these in my example logically should somehow be included within your newly established competency set.

This learning process is not about 'bad people or managers', which often might be an initial interpretation. Actually it is understanding our 'bad' practices and behaviors with not just leadership but in addressing work-relationships between individuals, leaders and departments. This is critical that people understand, because as you begin to focus on behaviors, it becomes personal.

This effort and process must include people realizing how 'we got here' and how we will go forward in rebuilding the workplace/organization - on ROCK this time!

THE PIECES... below is a brief description of each step or phase in this rebuilding process:

**The Organizational Leader [OL]**...President, Plant Manager, CEO, GM, etc

The success of any real endeavor to improve the organization's leadership, environment and culture must be led by the OL. His/her commitment and involvement will be absolutely critical to real change. The style, philosophy, beliefs, communication skills, etc of the one 'at the top' strongly influence the organization's culture and climate. This kind of Change Implementation in an organization takes a strong, secure leader, visionary...open to self-assessment, awareness and personal change! Is that you? ('kind of important', because YOU HAVE TO GO FIRST!)

REMINDER! This is all applicable to a business or independent team, staff, office, church (large/small), etc. As you work through this, consider the pieces that could apply to your own situation and how. Capturing some thinking right now could be a good idea:

The OL's Executive Leadership-Management Team

[ELMT] ...the top leadership team/level (VPs, Execs, Sr Staff, etc)

The management staff/team 'should' demonstrate teamwork that is the model for the rest of the organization. Power, territories and empires at the top often exist and create decisiveness downward affecting all other subordinate team efforts and necessary working-relationships. Frequently this is actually one of the worst teams in the organization. ELMTs are normally filled with aggressive, hard-charging, get-it-done-no-matter-what individuals that have reached those levels for precisely those reasons! Their individual performance and management may be effective; however interestingly enough, they never developed the skills required to function as a team-member (TEAMership). Egos and individualism must be realized, understood and fixed for this team to achieve higher levels of success.

LEADERSHIP-RELATIONSHIPS-TEAMERSHIP has to become what they are about – before moving downward into subordinate management.

 Visioning

A widely used and abused word that organizations attempt but most fail with executing. The visioning process and work frequently falls short and just ends up being a nice poster on a wall somewhere with little meaning. The visioning work here is that of each leader and each team working downward, envisioning what LEADERSHIP, RELATIONSHIPS and TEAMERSHIP would look like IF we could achieve. This seems minimal, but until people truly are on the same page, where we are going, and what it will/should look like, it is just the OL and maybe some consultant's vision! This process is critical as we move through each level of leadership and managers/supervision.

> 📖 Have you bought in and are you seeing the vision?

Establishment of Leadership Competencies

This is where 99% of all leadership development effort stops. It just never happens! Sure there may be training and development on some traits, skills and qualities, but then that training is not connected and therefore not reinforced back at the ranch. More often than not, during my initial years doing LEADERSHIP TRAINING, I was hired to come in to do leadership training according to *my own thinking/definition of what leadership was*.... It

30

was not training to a prescribed set of competencies that the organization decided and used with their leaders.

> 📖 Am I the only one that finds this strange, weird or what...to bring in an outsider to teach your people LEADERSHIP...as he/she sees leadership? Sure to HELP, but to do it all, anyway they wish?

Very likely your organization does precisely this, when/if they ever pursue management & supervisory development. However, we are here to focus on the SOLUTION - the organization must determine the traits/qualities, behaviors and skills (COMPETENCIES) for leadership to get established.

This is recommended to be accomplished with the OL and ELMT (with involvement and communication with all levels of leadership). We must determine those traits that we want in leaders, and these now will become our measuring stick for hiring, mentoring, training, firing, growing, promoting, etc.

LEADERSHIP PERFORMANCE COMPETENCIES

(…for use in mentoring, hiring, coaching, evaluation, feedback, performance, firing, training, promotion, etc…)

BUSINESS KNOWLEDGE (education, self-development, development of others, follower's knowledge, operational/technical…

COMMUNICATION SKILLS (counseling, listening, people informed, written/oral, expectations, presentation & facilitation skills, team communications, internal customers…

PROBLEM SOLVING / DECISION MAKING (judgment, conflict resolution, use of consensus, reasoning, creative…

SENSITIVITY (caring, respect, fairness, safety of people, understanding, supporting, loyalty, compassion, organizational support, approachable…

CHANGE FACILITATION (people empowered, open to other ideas, OK being wrong, open-minded, adaptive, flexibility, systems/process thinking, continuous improvement…

MOTIVATION (teaching, inspiring, charisma, growing people and teams, delegation, influence, turnover, involves people…

PRODUCTIVITY/RESULTS (making it happen, endurance, mission accomplishment, attainment of goals…

PLANNING and ORGANIZING (time management, plans, goals, dependability/reliability, controlling…

PROFESSIONALISM (appearance, accountable, presence, followership, standards, people skills, team-player, relationships, role model, tact...

ETHICS and VALUES (work ethic, honest, values, culture, integrity, admits mistakes...

> 📖 **NOTE:** Once again, it is not my intention to convince you that these are THE right competencies for you and/or your organization. The point here is that there needs to BE a set of competencies; your organization and its leaders/leadership must determine these.

 **Organizational / Team History, Baggage and Culture**

This is all about understanding where we have been, how we got here and what it has caused... It is imperative that we understand where our culture has been and what has made it the way it is. Past management and leadership practices determine where we (individuals and organizations) are today in our culture's morale and attitudes. This will also play into the difficulty of changing our culture. Poor leadership-practices and 'unskilled' managers in the past can have a very lasting effect on people. To regain the trust is not an easy thing... and we will have to gain it among the leaders and managers first. The relationship among the leaders from top to bottom, left to right, night/day shifts, etc all have to be right. It is important for leaders to understand that people have attitudes for very valid reasons. Typically they came from previous ineffective leadership, but it is yours now to understand and change!

 Supervisor Team / Frontline Leaders (FLL)

Most would agree that FLLs just might be the most important leadership roles within the entire organization due to their immediate impact on productivity and culture. Rarely, however do they get *any* developmental training for the skills that they now need (having moved from the most experienced, awesome Welder to now the Supervisor of the Welders)! Once again, we have people in places for 'what they know about welding' and experience. The skill-set that is now needed is very different (leadership skills and techniques). Some of the skills which typically need development are offered here for your thinking and consideration:

OUTCOMES, CONCEPTS, SKILLS and TOOLS (for leaders at all levels!):

- Understanding and realizing LEADERSHIP QUALITIES and TRAITS, the role of leaders
- TRUST...deeper understanding... building & breaking it.... the value of it.
- Understanding the Power of RELATIONSHIP-BUILDING.
- Going from PEER to LEADER.
- TEAM-BUILDING...how to...tearing it down...building it...understanding the need.

- MOTIVATION, ATTITUDE and MORALE.
- HUMAN NATURE and HUMAN BEHAVIOR.... understanding people and culture.
- Interpersonal COMMUNICATION...skills and techniques, barriers, improving.
- COMMUNICATION Systems and Processes within the organization...Chain of Command.
- CONFLICT, DISAGREEMENT and DIFFERENCES.... resolving and managing.
- Handling ideas, suggestions and input.
- LISTENING...a most powerful tool.
- BRAINSTORMING / TEAM PROB-SOLVING.
- CREDIT& PRAISE -RECOGNITION /REWARD.
- DISCIPLINE, COACHING and FEEDBACK.
- Handling negativism, COMPLAINTS
- Creating an Open and trusting environment.
- LEADERSHIP ASSESSMENT.... discovering 'where you stand'...levels of leadership.
- Group Dynamics, the impact that we have on each other, CONSENSUS and BUY-IN.
- MENTORING, COUNSELING and developing people.
- Presentation and FACILITATION tips/techniques.
- CONTINUOUS LEARNING, IMPROVEMENT and SYSTEMS-thinking.
- Understanding the concept of CHANGE...selling, processing and utilizing.
- DELEGATION ...skills and understanding (a great tool or a terrible one).

> 📖 Amazing huh...look at all that *'stuff'* that leaders should know!!! How could we possibly assume that anyone just possesses it all naturally?

← The Leadership TEAM / Chain of Command, (CofC)

Chain of command is a term typically attributed to the military and has negative connotations with many civilian workplaces. However, it is a lack of emphasis and discipline in how the chain-of-command functions that ironically works against the organization...as if it is something bad?!?

It determines how effective and consistent our leadership really is. When we skip levels of leadership (each other) for reasons of urgency, or convenience, we circumvent the CofC and other leaders. Subsequently, this grinds and erodes working relationships among members of the Leader team – the CofC. People (leaders) typically shrug their shoulders as if it is no big deal, but believe me, it actually is!

> 📖 It might be a good time to consider some things being said. What's on your mind? How does your Leadership Team/CofC function? Why?

*This occurs in all directions: the boss skipping you and going to one of your reports; or people jumping the CofC and going another level or two up to get resolution on some issue. We allow this so routinely; we become numb as to how much effect it really has on us; as well as its impact on communications and relations. Respect and relationships are damaged every time we allow and reinforce these 'everyday' occurrences. This is an area that causes major chaos, because everyone interprets how the CofC should work in a different way. This results in flawed practices with Open Door Policy, Skip-Level meetings (which should really go away), etc. Without solid CofC understanding, discussions and clarity, relationships are being damaged. Discipline (in our CofC practices) just might be a good thing!

Communication Processes/Systems and Barriers

In any organization where I have ever worked, this is easily the No#1 issue identified by the organization and folks within..."we need to be able to communicate more effectively". Once again, I look at leadership as the primary answer to this challenge. How does the Leadership Team - Chain of Command verbally communicate information in all directions? Do we rely on Human Resources (personnel office) to distribute information? Is it possible that we have become reliant on bulletin boards, memos, email, etc vs the verbal word? What are our communication processes and systems for information flow? Do we know where the barriers exist?

*** Over the last several years, I have also come to totally believe this: *Rarely is the issue really about ineffective communications, but rather it is about ineffective relationships.* Think about it!!!! Communicating is really fairly simple, yes some hiccups from time to time, but if the relationship is strong, the communicating will be also.

Organizational Trust and Relationships

This receives its own category of focus due to the importance it plays in how well we function and operate as a business family. Trust is a much deeper subject than most people even realize...it is so much more than just 'lying to people'. We are all in working-relationships that allow for constant opportunities to break promises with each other. Trust and relations among the leaders and chain-of-command need to be an initial focus, since we exhibit and demonstrate trust-levels to the rest of the organization. From top-down, this is where we will make the biggest difference if we are willing and committed to change. We must understand the impact that we have on each other...and how we break trust! Real change comes through *much* work in these areas. Once again, this is not so much a matter of character and integrity as it is about our 'communication practices', feedback and follow-through by leaders. [And no, this isn't just about some activity of falling back into someone's arms]

 Our Leadership Practices / Principles (what we are about)

The meaning of 'practices' here is how we conduct business within our People System. Some of these are: *Chain of command practices (as mentioned above)   *Open door policy (a killer to morale among leaders) *Decision-making and Problem-Solving at the lowest levels   * Consensus and Buy-in as a way of life.   *Communication practices (verbal, email, bulletin boards, memos, etc.)   *Disagreement is OK and encouraged. *Systems-thinking vs Firefighting...   *Role of leaders as facilitators vs dictators (see book, Teaching Fishing)   *Freedom to fail and risk taking *Feedback, conflict and confrontation are necessary for improvement, change and progress. *Leaders as coaches, teachers and mentors..... Etc, etc, etc. Bottom line here is that the CofC needs to spend time determining what we are about – what are the principles/practices that will define our leadership and culture?

Problem Solving, Decision-Making

Where are we as an organization? Are decisions and ideas generated from the top or are we an organization of consensus and buy-in at the lowest levels? Successful leaders and organizations are realizing how critical it is to change this direction of leadership. Competition demands that we no longer waste our most important resource and asset (people's thoughts). This is a critical mindset to develop in leaders at all levels that begins with the simple but constant question: "What do YOU think? What would YOU do?" Organizations and leaders that successfully develop this mindset, habit and culture will give people a sense of belonging and will ultimately make people want to work there. Teach 'em to fish! (From our first book, Teaching Fishing)

Learning Org. or Team / Handling Ideas

The knowledge held by an organization represents its intellectual capital. The knowledge that resides in an organization is the sum of everything that an organization knows (and that doesn't mean just a few know, the leader knows, etc)! It is the knowledge that gives it a competitive advantage – but only IF we systematically capture it and share with all.

- The focus lies in utilizing the talent, knowledge and technology as well as training resources to give all employees the best possible foundation to strive within the organization.
- New ideas and information are continuously infused into the organization. We must document changes as a matter of the

Change Process, which *all* understand as a necessity vs just being perceived as a useless drill and waste of time.

- Lastly, there needs to be a mindset of idea-generation being a good thing and something that is sought and wanted. It is a flow from the bottom-up! Ideas, solutions and changes should be a matter of the daily life of every individual, team and the entire chain of command. Leaders must facilitate this way of thinking.....annnnd, suggestion boxes need to go away! Why are we encouraging folks to put their thinking in a box on the wall? (Yes, I know, leaders don't care, there is no trust, and ideas are stolen, blah blah blah...). That's what we are after fixing and changing here, huh?

Change Implementation Strategy and Understanding

Dynamics of Change are hugely important to the successful leader, and to the success of an organization attempting to grow and get better. Leaders need to be taught and must understand the human relations-aspects involving change. People DO NOT 'naturally' resist change. Any resistance on people's part was not some natural occurrence but the result of past changes? This and any actual resistance is twofold, 1) past ineffective leadership in people's lives (parents, teachers, bosses, etc) who crammed change down people's throats; and 2) current leadership who continue to expect people to just buy-in and trust these sudden changes without involvement from the beginning. The successful organization is the one where leadership understands the CHANGE PROCESS and subsequently develops a process for all implementations. That process minimally must include:

- Allowing leadership to buy in first, from top to bottom...

- All people from top to bottom being given time to digest, gripe (as the leaders/execs were allowed to before buying in...) and understand...

- Communication planning for the entire implementation process...

- Taking any SURPRISE element out of the process...

- LEADERS being taught how to facilitate change with teams and people...

It turns out this last dynamic (about Change-processing) of our PIECES / THE DOZEN is a nice lead-in to a brief listing of bullets critical to the implementation of this book's Leadership Conversation - REBUILDING on ROCK!

IMPLEMENTING (FRAMEWORK)
...some considerations and thinking

- Each step, the immediate leader should help facilitate (when outside facilitators, trainers or consultants are used) - to eventually become *the* facilitator

- Every individual, of every team at every level, always working on their worst relationship

- There must be an understood need (vision) by all: INVOLVEMENT = COMMITMENT

- It will NOT happen overnight

- Competencies must be developed, bought into and evaluated routinely; behaviors WILL change when we are held accountable to a set of competencies

- Silos, territories, negative cliques and agendas not tolerated

- As we address 'fixing our people-system', we must make it the priority. Other change implementations, initiatives and programs should be to some degree put on the back-burner

- Nothing new, just hard work we must do and expect others to do; it is all about behavioral change

-

"Leaders always go first"
...every step of the way

So ...WHATCHATHINKIN?

WHAT WON'T DO IT!

(Programs, gimmicks, giveaways and broken promises of new beginnings…or these on their own…):

- Employee Day / Parking Spots
- Annual Picnic, Cookouts or Pizza parties
- Rewards and Recognition from top
- Promises of stuff, benefits, etc
- MBWA
- One-time programs: Cheese Moving, Fish Throwing etc
- Lunch with CEO
- Skip-level meetings
- Comp Time / Perfect Attendance programs
- Pay for Performance
- TEAM colors, names and banners
- (one-time) Workshops and Seminars
- Audio tapes, books, etc
- Townhall, the President speaks sessions
- Spirit Weeks / Diversity days
- Public Relations posters, signage
- GiveAways (t-shirts/pizza/etc)
- Surveys and Assessments
- Core Values / Mission Statement posters
- Consultants & Trainers …surprised ya' with this one huh?

📖 NOTE: None of these are 'bad things'. These can all be beneficial when they are attempted in addition to, supplementing and supporting an in-place effective leadership team.

> *"Effective Leaders realize they must get the Heart before Asking for the Hand"*
>
> …anonymous author

So that's it for our second book intended to be some solution ideas for you. I am sure you are THINKING by now, and now with our story (Part II), you will see these ideas attempted in application. This is the essence of what this book is about, a focus on what leading people is all about, and why many struggle with and maybe even hate managing people. For current managers, supervisors and yes, even the executives out there, the answer is very simple--you never learned how.

This story (and book) is about how to fix this dilemma and rebuild; individually or organizationally. Hope you enjoy it!

> 📖 Are you thinking? Consider capturing what is on your mind at this moment!

Part II

'REBUILDING On ROCK'

"Getting the New WORD Out..."

OUR STORY HERE (Part II) is about an organization called Tool Box Inc (TBI). TBI is like most any organization; every dynamic and every lesson here is applicable to most any organization or team. People, managers, management, culture, behaviors, conflicts, communication challenges, groups of people – collectively happening in *hopes* of achieving some result!

BACKGROUND FOR OUR STORY Some refresher about TBI, (discussed in detail in previous book 'Teaching Fishing' :

Booker is a new exec/VP at TBI, having joined the organization this past August. Booker is the Chief Leadership/Learning Officer (CLO); brought in specifically to fix organizational leadership. After much work with the CEO and the VP/Leadership Team over the past five months, the entire organizational chain of command has been gathered today. While the rest of the company (approximately 980 employees) has been given the day off – every Supervisor, Manager and Exec (73 to be exact) is here.

Booker was brought on board to take TBI to new levels, by improving the culture and creating leaders. The development of a sustainable LEADERSHIP DEVELOPMENT PROCESS was the ultimate goal. Today was time to 'get the WORD out' and begin the transformation. Leaders were going first!

TBI manufactures toolboxes — the kind that you see on the bed of pickup trucks. The company has been located in a small community just outside of

Kansas City, Missouri, for nearly 55 years. TBI is a very typical and traditional blue-collar company. Its workforce, like most, is made up of pretty good folks. Supervisors and managers typically achieve these positions because of their experience, seniority and expertise — like 95% of all organizations. Likely, this includes your organization, right? Yes, I know what you are thinking, and you are correct! Throughout the years, there were also a few supervisors and managers who had landed their positions because of *who they knew,* if you know what I mean. I'm guessing you do. Some of those could be found even at the top of the chain of command. This is no longer how things will be done however.

OK, so that catches us up a bit and leads us to our story and today!

The CLO (Booker) speaks to LEADERSHIP TEAM...

The sun shone brightly on the snow, one early January day. An additional three inches had come down last night, and there were still light flurries as people rolled into the auditorium. In concert with the brightness of the sun and the snow, there was optimism in the air as TBI was beginning a new year. As most of us (and organizations as well), tend to think - it is a good time for 'new beginnings'. It is also a time of the year that companies like to 'roll out' new programs, initiate changes, renew commitments, make promises, etc! Booker and the CEO knew what was being launched this morning would be taken this way (as just another fire-them-up program). Booker, along with the senior leaders and the CEO knew for sure that this was *not* just some program of the month. The difference this time, people would discover, was that this was the early stages of a never ending long-term process. This wasn't about fixing *them* (the employees/workforce), it was about leaders changing. Real leadership would become the new reality – a new way of doing business. From the top, they were committed to making it happen. This would be *a new beginning in the middle* of the life of the organization - REBUILDING this place on ROCK this time! Blue skies were ahead, but there would definitely be some fog, storms and cloudiness encountered along the way. TBI had an absolute focus on the PEOPLE SYSTEM, as Booker liked to refer to it. The relationships and leadership of individuals and among all groups, shifts, departments and offices was the focus - beginning with every leader. This would begin with the individual leader and his team, at the top – the CEO! All would hear this morning how this process had begun a few months back, with the leaders at the top, going first.

It was indeed cold and icy outside, as it typically is in the Midwest this time of year. There was a bit of a chill inside as well, but there was also plenty of coffee and hot chocolate available. The talk, focus on personal behavior and 'visioning' getting ready to happen would undoubtedly also help to warm things up. This was no motivational gig, but a morning devoted to and focusing on each person there - new expectations regarding performance and behavioral change.

The downtown bakery had messed up the order, creating a bit of a shortage with the goodies, pastries and donuts that were being provided. With a bit of creativity however (cutting them in half, etc), all would be fed. This shortage had Booker trying to formulate a way to fit it into today's talk to the leaders. The 'feeding of the multitudes' from biblical scriptures, could be connected somehow, he thought to himself. Maybe he could somehow present some parallels, maybe not. The donut distribution…the feeding of the multitudes by Jesus and…the multiplication dynamic that would occur when we had real leadership and teamwork happening at TBI. There was a neat parallel in there somewhere Booker mumbled to himself. When we have RELATIONSHIPS, LEADERSHIP and TEAMERSHIP happening, how much more could we do (or produce)? This was about the synergy, the use of everyone's input, a happy workforce and all that sort of thing. Creating that vision was the primary goal today!

He wasn't sure if he could fit it in, but what he was sure of was that someday soon, PEOPLE would become our MOST VALUABLE RESOURCE was going to become a reality. This process, he thought to himself, was similar to Jesus transforming the seemingly small amount of bread and fish into well.........LOTS!

So, the organizational leadership of TBI was gathered; the CEO would be here shortly. He was running a bit late after having to deal with an 'all-nighter' hospital emergency with a grandchild (that he and his wife were raising). Today was important and although the executive group had encouraged him (the CEO) to not come in, he was coming. This was something that he could not miss.

The exec team had been working and strategizing on this 'rebuilding of leadership' effort for months. Not just that, but the CEO and team at the top had indeed changed much in terms of their own behaviors. These efforts had even seen one VP go away, not being willing to change and focus on all this 'warm and fuzzy' stuff as he called it. It was definitely for the best, and the replacement, the new VP of Inventory/Shipping, Ms. Ruth had been a great addition to the 'new team'. This would indeed be part of the message today - to get all to realize the commitment to this process, from the top! It would require leaders to change, all of us. There would be plenty of help and resources provided to help each and every one, but there needed to be little doubt in folk's minds that you were going to be expected to change. REAL LEADERSHIP would be learned and expected; and RELATIONSHIPS would become a priority or likely 'you would also go away'.

> 📖 What could effective leadership, relationships and teamership mean to your own team and/or within in your organization?

> 📖 How much more product could be made or services be provided if ALL were behind the efforts?

Most were in their seats in the enormous auditorium that TBI had added onto the plant 12 years ago. Mr. Fisher (founder/owner) had wanted a place to bring large groups together, as well as giving the community a multi-purpose facility for community events. It had been kept in great condition, to include upgrading current technology in terms of projectors, audio equipment, PowerPoint capabilities, etc. The CEO had made that all happen in a short period of time, after taking the reins as the new CEO. Mr. Matthews, who had been a janitor from the first days of TBI, now carried the title of Maintenance & Facilities Engineer, took special care of this place. He took a lot of pride in keeping it nice for all. He was speaking with Booker and ensuring the PowerPoint and audio was all working as the final folks settled into their seats. Just then, Booker boomed into the microphone, "Good morning and Happy New Year". The place got the hint, chatter began to subside and the place went quiet, as Booker continued, "We have a couple of changes, messing with the timing, but I think we have them under control. By the way, I hope all had a great Christmas and the Good Lord blessed you and your family over the holidays. I will assume all received the Christmas present I mailed each and every one of you?" Booker grinned hugely as they all knew he was just messing with them and a few joked back with him with comments of how it must have been lost in the mail, did you get mine, not too late, blah, blah, blah.

Booker went on, "Well let's get on with it. I have asked a good friend of mine, a leader in his own industry and a friend in Faith, Dr. K or Doc as most of us call him, to kick this important day off for us. Doc has a passion for leadership, teaching, preaching learning...and you are going to be seeing him around here. We have asked the 'good doctor' to share with us one of his Affirmations - which he writes, creates, distributes and yes, even sings! I am sure it will set the tone, create the mood and get us focused a bit. Because Dr. K has to hit the road early this morning to get back to Wisconsin, we have to let him do his thing and kick him out of here. Doctor it's all yours." He reached out shaking hands and grabbed the microphone from Booker, "Good morning to each and every one of you. I hope your time this morning focusing on one my favorite topics, LEADERSHIP, is a blessed time and plenty of learning and new thoughts and ideas will occur as you begin 2010. As Book said, I do have to hit the road quickly. Before I leave, I want to share a few words with you. Today, you will hear a lot of *stuff* as Book likes to call it. The key to getting something out of what you will hear today is to know, understand, and accept that you are being given wisdom…wisdom that will lead you along a path of true and strong leadership. The words I will leave with you today are titled, "The Benefits of Wisdom". Please know I will see you all again and here's to a productive day, full of learning!"

As he began singing, the words were scrolled upon the screen:

Slide #1

Lord, I praise and thank you for the
Benefits of your wisdom.
Because of my life in you,
You have forgiven me of all my sins and
Have healed me of my sicknesses.
You have provided me with your direction in the word and
teachings you send each day.

Each day, I keep your commandments in my heart and
make them a part of who I am.
I live a life that is full of faith and
Show love to all I encounter.

I walk in true victory and rebuke the
Influence of the enemy against me
And my family.
I walk each day without condemnation and
I win favor and a good name
In the sight of men.

Lord, I trust in you with all of my heart.
I do not turn to the right or to the left
Using my own judgment.
I lean totally on you and your wisdom knowing that all I
achieve is because
And the result of you.

As I walk, lean, and trust on you,
I know you will show your ever-abounding love to me; you
will prolong my life and
Prosper me mightily.
And you will keep me on my straight path that grows from
the benefits of your wisdom!   Amen.

At 'Amen', pretty much everyone was on his/her feet applauding, Doc had quite an impressive voice; some were even fighting back tears. The anticipation of today's focus along with holiday emotions was on folk's minds, causing some feelings to come out. It had definitely been an emotional year – not the least was the campaign to prevent the plant from unionizing early last year! Yes leadership was needed here for sure. The rumors of Hope, Promise and Change were in the air, and maybe it was possible to return to times when people felt part of a family here at TBI.

Doc waved to the crowd, embracing Book with a hug as they passed on the stage, and was gone behind the curtains. People were sensing something good might be happening here…

Booker, fully 'miked-up' with headset on, wandered across the stage smiling and gesturing to the crowd to settle down. The projector clicked and the first visual of the day was being shown on the enormous projector screen:

Slide # 2

"PEOPLE DON'T CARE HOW MUCH YOU KNOW, UNTIL THEY FIRST KNOW HOW MUCH YOU CARE."

Booker began, "Thanks again to our good friend who has truly set the stage with those words, nice voice huh?" He continued on without pause, "I am giving you each a copy of the words he shared with you. There is much there to digest, so I strongly recommend you hang onto them and read through them again soon. I have also included a scripture reference that relates to Doc's affirmation. For those of you taking notes, it is based on the Word from Psalm 103: 1-3 and Proverbs 3: 2-6.

OK, soooooo, what are we doing here this morning?" A new slide was projected on the big screen:

Slide #3

'REBUILDING on ROCK'

　　　RELATIONSHIP
+　　LEADERSHIP
+　　TEAMERSHIP
=　　'a REBUILT CULTURE'

"Gang, this is the beginning of a new way of existing here at TBI. This existence and new way will begin with you and I; all 70 of us right here right now. Today and our future is about the *changed* leaders of TBI! Let me assure you that this is about YOU and me and all those sitting around you, and not someone else. It is about behavioral change; learning new ways to effectively take care of people and each other; and well, creating a new organization rebuilt on rock! The rock I am speaking of here is about strong relationships, real leadership and ultimately a caring team-culture. In case this concept isn't clear to you, this *rock deal* originates from the bible, Matthew 7:25", as he looked to the screen…

Slide #4

The rain came down, the streams rose,
And the winds blew
And beat against that house;
Yet it did not fall,
Because it had its foundation
On the rock.

"…this 'foundation of rock' equates to our situation totally. If we have strong leadership, committed bonds and strong relationships among us, then we are solid and can withstand challenges and problems that arise. Conversely, when we are built on sand, when we don't have effective leadership; conflicts, agendas and territories exist. When relationships are not solid, then we erode and don't function well - to say the least (as a new slide hit the screen). And yes gang, this is *us* right now. It is what holds us back from being AWESOME:

Slide #5

- Micro-managing leaders vs leaders that involve and ask others their thoughts
- Bottlenecks within teams in the form of conflicts
- Baggage between individuals/groups
- People jumping the chain of command/skipping over others to get the answer they want
- People wanting to be right vs getting the right/best answer to problems
- People talking about others
- Territories, Silos, Agendas of individuals and departments
- The top leadership team is not modeling

"You are getting my point here?" Booker began slowly strolling across the stage deliberately giving people time to think. He then pointed at the screen clicking the remote to bring up:

Slide #6

"But everyone who hears these words of mine

And does not put them into practice is like a

foolish man who built his house on sand."

As the murmuring settled, he turned back toward the audience and continued, "Let me share a story with you, my story. Before I do, I want you to know that although at first it may seem that way, what I am sharing is not about me. This is about *you and all* of us, and the road to how we got here – where we are today. This is about the journey we are all getting ready to take – of how leadership is developed and our organization becoming about leadership. One more point here, what we are getting ready to focus on and all of our future talks, mentoring, training, development and work are *not* about anyone being a bad person. It is hugely important that you hear this! Hear me again, this is not about you or any other leaders here being bad, but it is about bad leadership practices. And FYI, all organizations deal with this dynamic. However we won't look like the rest of them someday soon. Let me get on with it.

This time with all of us, was actually planned about five months ago. First we had to allow time for the CEO, myself and the other VPs to *begin* 'walking' a different walk around here. We all realize we are *not there yet*! However until we began to change and developed a better understanding of leadership, we couldn't jump right in and start talking. We couldn't tell you something or preach at you about behaviors 'that we were not'.

The following PowerPoint, with some *bells and whistles*, began to fade onto the screen:

Slide #7

You <u>can't not</u>
'LEAD BY EXAMPLE'!
...think about it...

I would rather <u>see</u> a sermon
Than <u>hear</u> one any day...
I'd rather you would walk with me,
Than merely show the way...
The lectures you deliver
May be very wise and true,
But I think I'll get my lesson
By watching what you do...
Because I might misunderstand you,
And all the high advice you give,
But there's no misunderstanding
How you act and how you live

We are <u>ALWAYS</u>...
'LEADING BY EXAMPLE'
...think about it...!

Anonymous author

We are actually hoping you have already begun to see *some* different *walking* among us. We are accountable to be the first to change, followed by all of you. Today we are simply beginning the visioning process of where we are going. This is <u>where we are going</u>, in our future, beginning now. It is time to clarify new expectations and to talk about how we as the leaders, will start becoming accountable to the organization and your people – to lead.

OK, so please bear with me, while I share my story and how I got here... Why I think the way I do... Why I preach what I do... Hang in there and I believe you will see why I am sharing this momentarily; and connect it to *how you got here.*

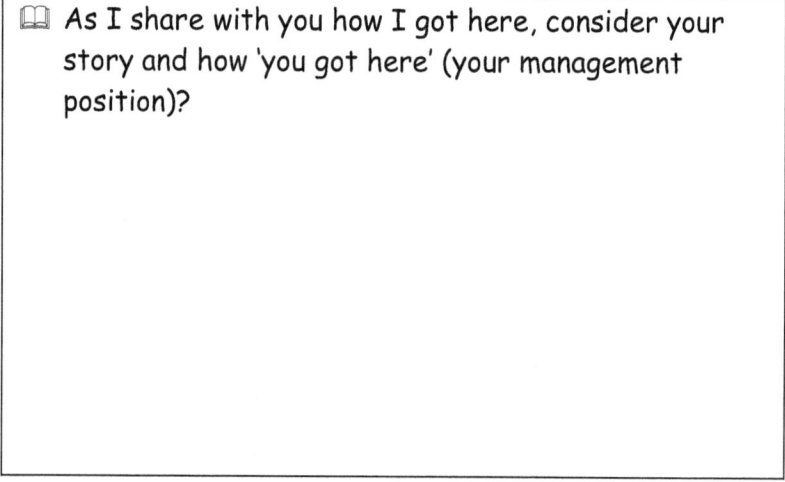

So here's the deal - I view myself as having grown up in a bit of a 'Leave it to Beaver' environment - great parents, family, friends, small town and all. Not rich or wealthy except for the life itself. I loved growing up in Lexington, a small community near here along the Missouri River, on the east side of KC. Some forty years ago or so, I was heading to college with my goal of becoming a teacher and coach, in probably a high school setting. Funny enough, even though I do coach, mentor and teach today, that has been all with the adult-learning population. I never did teach or coach in the school (secondary) as intended, and boy am I glad, because I totally love working with adults.

During my college time, I became involved with ROTC (Reserve Officer Training Corps) and ended up going off to the Army after graduating college. I spent my next 15 years as an Army Infantry Officer, retiring in 1992 as a Major; taking a buy-out/severance deal the military was offering during a military drawdown.

It was good timing for me as I had kids entering their middle-school years. I never liked the thought of moving them around during their high school years, so this was a good thing in many ways. So we took the money and ran. I had served God and Country, which I had considered was a good benefit about this whole military experience. Well anyway, back to our story - this leadership thing and the point to all this.

As I was leaving the military, I was sending out resumes with the 'thinking' that I would sell my LEADERSHIP and MANAGEMENT skills, experience and qualifications. I clearly saw leadership as a skill set. As I was soon to find out, that wasn't how the rest of the world dealt with leadership.

> 📖 **WHAT DO YOU THINK? What was happening here?**

As I remember back, it seemed what I was hearing, was essentially "yeah, we see all this on your resume, but what can you DO?" Having commanded three times and led other smaller units, I was a bit perplexed at that point. I began to realize that although the military takes a leader through all kinds of leadership development before giving command responsibility of a soldier (or employee) - the rest of the world didn't seem to work that way! Leadership was not a skill or trait in itself, hummmmmm?

Fortunately I had the luck of connecting with a local university in Jonesboro, Arkansas where I had settled after separating from the military. The local university's Continuing Education Dept was looking for a Leadership/Management Trainer. For the next couple of years, I headed down a road of doing lots of managerial and supervisory training programs for companies in various industries. This was comfortable, challenging and something I had become passionate about – Learning, Teaching/Training, Behavioral change and yes, Leadership for sure. I had done a fair amount of all of this during my time as a ROTC Instructor at Kansas State University near the end of my career. It was there that I became passionate about facilitating, coaching, mentoring, teaching…and yes developing leaders and leadership!

After these first few years of training with business and industry, something was not feeling right. I knew I was doing a good job, but was I really helping this organization in a sustainable way (training their frontline supervisors/mid-level managers)?"

Booker at this point, asked them to process the question and the story thus far, with those around them. He gave them some time to converse with those seated around them, to stretch a bit, and think, while he sipped his coffee.

> 📖 **Any guess what is wrong with this picture?**

As he gestured for them to wrap up their talks and get quiet again, one of Booker's managers was all over this question, his hand waving back and forth. Booker spotted it, subsequently asking him for his thoughts, "What are you thinking Bob?"

Bob blurted out, "What about *their* bosses, their managers? What did *they* know about leadership?"

Booker, smiling, responded, "You all realize that Bob had a bit of an edge on you all in answering this. I have been talking leadership to my guys for several months now and they know this story. But anyway, let me expand on this a bit." Booker continued, "What I was hearing from those participants in leadership develop programs, I like to phrase this way,

'…that's great stuff Booker but we don't do that *here'*, or words to that affect, …or maybe words like these, 'my boss is the one that needs to be here' and other such words…

68

You see what was going on in training wasn't being reinforced back at the ranch. There was no accountability to practice and change behavior back in the workplace. People were thinking to themselves about what they were returning to after training!

> 📖 Let's say that you just learned about CONSENSUS in management training and go back to work with the same boss practicing management the same old way. He/she comes to you and asks about a decision regarding my operation. I think: go talk to my team, listen to them, get their opinion, gain consensus, etc. However as I turn to go; my boss wants my answer now. He/she is expecting me to always have the answer. What is being created here?

OK, so let me tell you what I was hearing and learning from participants in training", Booker rolled onward, "They were confused with the messages from training and what was being reinforced from an opposite direction back at the ranch? I can see by most of your expressions that you understand, and right you are. Their boss was asking them to NOT do what was just learned; but rather what was just learned NOT to do. This is the challenge and dilemma faced with leadership development. The reality is that most of our practices and ways of managing folks create ineffective management and micro-managers!

Micro-managing! You might be thinking, why? We have you thinking huh? So think about it - this is important to understand about where we are today as managers here at TBI!

You see, if I have to always have the answer ready, in keeping my boss happy, I have to micro-manage and spend my time *in my people's stuff*! And oh yeah, all those benefits to doing things in a consensus-way, my people won't be getting. You see, I am not practicing listening, involving, asking opinions, respecting the team thought, making people feel important, creating thinkers and a sense of belonging!

And my people will just go on muttering, 'well that training didn't do any good. It looks like the same old manager/supervisor to me'. He/she/they will be right. Meanwhile time will go by and those training materials, content and *intent* will just be sitting on a shelf gathering dust. No behavioral change has happened, since there is no accountability to change back at the ranch. You have likely had these thoughts about leaders of yours in the past, and trust me; your people have them about *you* as well. For many you, they are thinking this way about you right now. We have been causing and reinforcing that dynamic from the top down. No longer my friends, no longer! Over a couple of year's period, I discovered a lot about what organizations do and don't do regarding management. One key dynamic was that leadership was a top-down learning process. Additionally that hiring, teaching, growing, training, promoting, and developing supervisors and managers in LEADERSHIP is one thing they *don't* do. And yes, what you are thinking right now is correct. This includes us here at TBI as well. We don't hire, promote or recognize management for leadership *stuff*, but rather for results you can drive your team to produce any way you can. This may not seem all that out of whack until you really think and understand what your team *could* produce if led effectively.

My belief along with my fellow VPs and your CEO here at the top, is that the possibilities could be astronomical and the sky is the limit. Again, IF we had this organization built on rock – what more could we do and be? What do you think *your* team could do if every relationship was strong; the conflicts and people issues were resolved; leadership was happening and problems/decisions were made by all? Picture you and the entire team having full buy-in versus your current state of affairs? Likely right now you are doing most everything with only half of the team truly behind the effort - because only half of the team made the decision? Think of it this way. If a 'perfect team' was equal to a ten on a scale of one to ten, at what number would you say your team is currently functioning?

> 📖 ...and YOURS?

OK, so you see my point? In my experiences, with no leadership development in place, most teams are actually somewhere between a five and seven, or so. Now if you want to sit there and be bold and say it is at a seven, what would it mean if you could get it to maybe 8.5 or a nine? And how do we get each and every team here to an 8, 9 or 10? Right you are – the difference makers are LEADERSHIP, TEAMERSHIP & RELATIONSHIPS! Pardon my French, but what would it mean if we could get rid of the crap that exists everywhere between individuals, departments, shifts, office staffs and groups of people throughout our organization? How many more toolboxes could we produce? How might that affect our turnover? How many more smiles would we see around here? What would a lot of smiles mean to us? How much better would our quality be? How many people would be coming to work content vs. looking for work elsewhere? How many of our problems would really be solved? How much easier would change be implemented?"

Booker waited for the pause and silence he was sure would happen at this point. He strolled around on the stage, letting people think for a moment as he strolled halfway across the stage before continuing.

"You see, TBI is just like maybe 99% of organizations in our society that do not develop leadership before placing someone in a leadership role. This leadership dilemma has become the norm in the society; we are going to fix it at TBI, beginning today.

Persistence & commitment will be required...

And an attitude of:

"Failure is not an Option"

...from the Apollo13 mission/movie

As I mentioned previously and you will hear it said again and again as we go forward, leadership is not just about what you know about toolboxes, any more. Just then he clicked his remote device and his favorite quote was on the big screen:

> Slide # 2 (again)
>
> ## "PEOPLE DON'T CARE HOW MUCH YOU KNOW, UNTIL THEY FIRST KNOW HOW MUCH YOU CARE."

Suffice it to say that letting people know you care, and demonstrating that caring is important. It will become the leader's norm. This attitude along with developing ourselves through a set of Leadership Competencies will become our competitive edge. We will begin measuring ourselves according to some skills, traits and behaviors that *might* look like these (as he clicked on the next slide). These are not determined yet, just intended to be a sample of what our competencies might look like. We will develop these together, the 70 of us!

Slide #8

LEADERSHIP PERFORMANCE COMPETENCIES
(For use in mentoring, hiring, coaching, evaluation, feedback, performance, firing, training, promotion, etc)

BUSINESS KNOWLEDGE (education, self-development, development of others, follower's knowledge, operational/technical...

COMMUNICATION SKILLS (counseling, listening, people informed, written/oral, expectations, presentation & facilitation skills, team communications, internal customers...

PROBLEM SOLVING / DECISION MAKING (judgment, conflict resolution, use of consensus, reasoning, creative...

SENSITIVITY (caring, respect, fairness, safety of people, understanding, supporting, loyalty, compassion, organizational support, approachable...

CHANGE FACILITATION (people empowered, open to other ideas, OK being wrong, open-minded, adaptive, flexibility, systems/process thinking, continuous improvement...

MOTIVATION (teaching, inspiring, charisma, growing people and teams, delegation, influence, turnover, involves people...

> ***PRODUCTIVITY/RESULTS*** (making it happen, endurance, mission accomplishment, attainment of goals...
>
> ***PLANNING and ORGANIZING*** (time management, plans, goals, dependability/reliability, controlling...
>
> ***PROFESSIONALISM*** (appearance, accountable, presence, followership, standards, people skills, team-player, relationships, role model, tact...
>
> ***ETHICS and VALUES*** (work ethic, honest, values, culture, integrity, admits mistakes...

The reason I shared *my story* with you was not to make you believe that the military is the greatest organization in the world. However LEADERSHIP and what I call growing TEAMERSHIP is something they grasp and practice as a way of life – something we can learn from, huh? You see, before I ever took a soldier (or employee) under my wings as the leader, I had tons of repetitious leadership training and learning. Of course yes, I could have still become an ineffective leader, but at least I had a prayer of success! Now consider what we have done TO YOU, and those you lead, in preparing you for your leadership job? Trust me it's the same thing that 99% of organizations have done to their management folks. Every leader around you, was not given that position based upon leadership, but rather on being a *know it all,* about making toolboxes. Ooooh that kind of hurts huh?" Booker grinned big to assure them that he understood this pain, and to keep the learning mood in place.

"But it also explains some things about you, your peers, your boss and our chain of command right here huh?" There was a quiet hush over the group of leaders, and Booker allowed the silence to go on a few minutes. The fact that everyone's boss was sitting there in this very same conversation made it even quieter…

> 📖 ARE YOU QUIETLY THINKING RIGHT NOW AS WELL?

"You get it don't you? We are beginning a journey and process today to address this. Within the coming months and years, we will no longer be like those 99%-ers!

Here's just a bit more about what we are up against and intend to fix. Consider that the military moves people around consistently; if I walk in as your leader, I better have some leadership abilities, skills and understanding. Now in our world at TBI, we are trying to sell our people on 'how much I know about toolboxes' being the same as leadership. This isn't leadership, and that doesn't work, does it? Think of it this way – the organization (civilian or military) was performing acceptably before the new leader got there, to some degree. What I *should* be expected to do as the new leader, is provide leadership and improve/make things better…not just maintain. When you take over as a manager or supervisor at TBI, does your team need more years of tool box experience and knowledge or leadership? Consider that most teams here have on average about 95 years of toolbox experience and expertise.

Lastly, just something to kick around -it's also kind of interesting how our civilian world uses terms like MANAGER where the military tends to not distance itself from the word LEADERSHIP! Maybe we will consider some title changes down the road as well, huh? However let's change our behaviors first!

> 📖 Kind of amazing, but some organizations have actually attempted to change all this by simply changing the titles of their supervisors/managers!

> 📖 Have you experienced or heard of that, as a solution to fixing leaders?

Hey gang, I have given you a lot that I want you to ponder and process, so let's take a short break. See you back here for Round#2 in a few moments."

> Slide #9
>
> **_Another favorite sarcastic quote of mine, <u>about leaders and leadership</u>_**
>
> *"I'm not BOSSY,*
> *I just have better ideas..."*
>
> *** Think about it ***

This quote was lit up on the screen as people returned from the break and settled back into their seats. Some chuckling began as all began spotting it and pointed it out to buddies. Booker hollered, "Happy New Year!...let me just take you a step or two further in understanding where we are going with all this. Consider this quote up on the screen right now, and how when we promote people into leadership roles for 'what they know', we are setting them up to lead with their only known strength. The fact that they know more than anyone else; in fact we are setting you up to practice leadership according to this quote in many ways! I know some of you are *resembling* this remark huh? You have discovered that all the technical and operational know-how doesn't quite do it for those you lead, does it? They want this other stuff that no one ever taught you huh? I tend to call that *stuff* – LEADERSHIP!!! If I am there for my wisdom and smarts, I likely don't even realize I am modeling this quote. I just in fact consciously or subconsciously believe that I do have better ideas because I am the smartest one here; and we all know that because that's how I got here. Chew on that one for a moment."

After a few moments, Booker gestured toward the screen, with one bullet at a time being displayed...

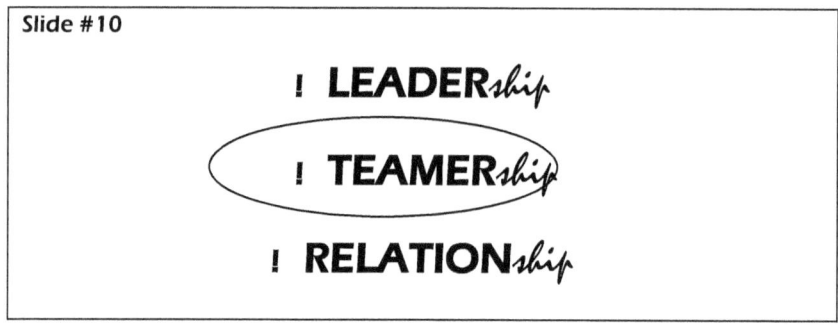

Slide #10

He used his laser pointer in placing a red dot on the screen and circled the word TEAMership over and over, "Does anyone have a guess what this term possibly could be about?" After some suggestions, hitting all over it, Booker continued, "No biggee, just a term I dreamed up or stole somewhere and I like to use as an attention-getter as much as anything. I use it to communicate that it as a skill set just as LEADERSHIP is its own skill set. It is about the skills required to work together with others. You see we actually do the same thing with TEAMership that we do with LEADERSHIP - we assume everyone possesses this *stuff* as well. I won't get much more into this right now, but just let me add this to your thinking and our discussion. The first efforts in TEAMership will come with this group of leaders' right here. Everyone here is on a team with peers, other leaders – team mates, right? How are those relationships? What are we modeling as teams of leaders here? I know you know where I am going, huh? Exactly. One of our first steps in this never-ending process of Rebuilding on Rock will be rebuilding not only your own LEADERSHIP SKILLS, but also the RELATIONSHIPS within your management teams. That's TEAM-ership, and we have some work to do in that regard.

Let me share this with you. The CEO and our VP-leadership team have been working on precisely this over the last six months, our TEAMership! As I mentioned earlier, we had one casualty in rebuilding this team, losing a longtime manager here at TBI. He chose to go and that may well be a choice some of you may make. When we hold you accountable to not just get along and communicate, but to actually improve your relations with each other...some of you might just consider jumping this ship. It is absolutely not what we hope for, but it will be a choice of yours. You see our relationships are important and critical to this rebuilding. Consider this: how do we lead people and hold them accountable to get along and build relationships with their team members, when we, their leaders don't practice these things? Again, it is why this team of VPs had to go first with all this, and our relationships are vastly improved compared to a few months back.

If you think about it, the VP team *should* be the model team for the organization; and that is our plan. We may not yet be the best yet, but I know for sure that we no longer are the worst. My belief and the others can speak for themselves, is that about five months ago, we were indeed very possibly one of the worst teams at TBI. This dynamic is totally normal for those 99% of organizations we spoke about earlier.

> 📖 How about the organization where you work or those others you have belonged to?

But just as I said we weren't going to be in that 99% anymore, this team at the top won't be either. Interestingly enough, the military provides a model for this as well. It may be a stretch and for some of you that were in the military and went through Basic Training, you may not have thought of it as TEAM-training, but wasn't it? I know some of you are thinking of your Basic Training with possibly other colorful terminology, but essentially it is in place to break down individualism and promote the value, attitude and provide teamwork-skills. And why do they do this?

They realize that all people came from various backgrounds, dysfunctional friends/families possibly and an individually-focused educational society. It might be smart to teach TEAMership and not just assume everyone has people-skills and is an effective team player!

Just as we are going to have competencies to really address Leadership, we are also going to develop a connecting set of competencies for being hired here as an employee! We are not just after the best Welder we can find, but the best Welder that also has TEAMership skills. Again, you may struggle with how we will do this, but just know this – we will figure it out. Leaders will learn, practice and be evaluated on leadership; and employees will learn, practice and be evaluated based upon a set of 'employee/team player traits'. This process will be how we begin creating a pipeline of leadership here - where leadership dynamics are the focus from the day we are hired.

Now, once again, let's be clear, that LEADERS GO FIRST. We must fix *us* first, again from the top down. Then as leaders begin to change and practice leadership, they will begin growing their people based on expectations we will have determined regarding what we want in our people, workforce and culture.

> 📖 So what are you thinking?

Let me address a concern I have heard through the years, anywhere and everywhere that I have shared, taught and practiced these beliefs of leadership. Likely some of you are thinking and wondering about this as well.

Here's the argument, 'Aren't these traits, competencies, behaviors and people skills subjective? Can you really measure them? Many of these are just who we are, they are personality stuff. You can't fairly evaluate managers on these personal qualities can you?' Some of you are thinking this, right? Let's consider this a bit more deeply. Let me ask you this – don't we all evaluate and judge others all the time on these supposedly *immeasurable dynamics*? We measure our friends, our co-workers, management overall, our boss, and other people in leadership roles in our worlds.

Think about it for a moment. As we all would think about what we want in our leader, which is much of what we looked at moments ago, don't we very easily and quickly make assessments of our leaders based on these things, these criteria, flaws, competencies, etc?

Well if this is the case, and I think you all are agreeing with this, then shouldn't we be developing and growing leaders based on what people want and need in their leader and leadership? If it is what we want in our leader and in leadership, why don't we grow leaders according to these competencies?

Now I realize this is all hard to digest, because it has not been 'our way' officially over well, pretty much our entire lives! However *how* you play the game is indeed now going to be evaluated on the same level as the final score. Work on that one for a moment! Just getting results and knowing more than anyone else is not LEADERSHIP anymore. While you were producing results, maybe by yourself and the couple of others on your team that were doing it all, what was going on with the other 50-75% of your team? Giving marginal effort, complaining about you and coworkers while hoping to land a job somewhere other than here?

> 📖 Sound like your team, and workplace?

Achieving productivity and getting the job done by a relatively small portion of your team or department is not going to fly anymore. Leaders are here to grow people and teams. A team that is totally involved, all inputting, all satisfied, all with buy-in, all wanting to come back to work tomorrow, etc.

The excuses of 'every team having a couple of bad apples,...... people will just be people,... overlooking conflicts,... allowing bad relationships' is no longer acceptable. That is what we call management, just maintaining the status quo or what is there. That's managing and not leading! You see, leaders fix, improve, make better and ultimately are builders in all ways; this fixing is not just about operations, but it is about FIXING PEOPLE SYSTEMS also.

As you process this a bit in your head, also realize that the days where we tried to lead your people from up here, from the top, are done. We are not going to count on motivational speakers, giveaway programs, empowerment committees, CEO rah-rah talks, Christmas holiday hams or other gimmicks. The CEO is not the leader of your people, you are. Trust me; he has plenty to do in leading the eight of us up here! We are *his* team, *your* people are not. Now, don't panic. Just as we didn't get here overnight, we won't fix this overnight. What this is all about here today is creating a vision. Are you seeing the picture? This is indeed where we are going. You will get on the bus or you won't.

This is about each and every one of us in our leadership learning and growing. It is a development process to begin becoming leaders, and not being OK with just being an effective manager. This will happen from the top down, let me assure you. All of us here at the top realize that we are the first that must learn and begin practicing these competencies; and being held accountable for them. As I have already told you, this has already begun. As we begin to change, and truly understand leadership, we will begin that development of these competencies down through the chain of command. Now if that sounds like a long time to get *there*, it is. This is a system and process that must be done right. While it may take a bit for your own leader or boss to begin really changing, you don't have to wait. Start focusing on these competencies and discussing them with your own people. Begin creating open-ness and seeking input from your people/your team on how *you* are doing as their leader? Can you do this? Likely this seems a bit scary and probably some of you won't attempt this. Over time, you will. It will become our way of life with every leader and his/her team and people.

We are headed for a day where every leader from the day of hiring, will have these competencies in their face, with a clear expectation and accountabilities. The day will also come when it may not be the most technically competent person on the team!

> 📖 How does that one grab you?

Likely that kind of rubs you wrong, huh? Realize this; LEADERSHIP KNOWLEDGE is getting ready to become re-defined. Rebuilding each of us and all of us is what this New Year is all about... Before I let you go, this all seems probably even weird and maybe unrealistic, since you have never been anywhere in your existence where your personal behaviors were really judged and evaluated – at least not in a productive way. Anytime your behavior was discussed was likely by other people in the break room or when you were getting chewed out because some behavior wasn't acceptable. And likely that came after a long time of doing that behavior and only when things got really bad, right? We will reach a point where we are going to address behavior on the spot when it happens—and that interaction will be a good thing. You see, and I will hit on this more shortly, we have to turn around our thinking on feedback, and become about 'constructive criticism' being a way of life...timely, real, helpful, and tactfully delivered and for positive reasons. You see, when we improve behaviors, not only do you get better, so does the team and the organization. OK enough for now, get out of here and go relax for a bit."

📖 What are you thinking?

> Slide #11
>
> # THAT WAS THE *PHILOSOPHY.*
>
> # ...NOW SOME ABSOLUTE
>
> # *PRINCIPLES*

"Ok so our first couple of hours here were all about creating a vision, some big picture stuff and some philosophy. Before we begin wrapping up the day with the CEO before lunch, let me share with you some absolutes that WILL BE non-negotiable for our culture as leaders. As I mentioned previously, what we specifically measure, and what those exact competencies are, will be something *we* will develop with consensus from all.

However the stuff I am going to describe here *will be* our new culture. It *will* be what you are and what you walk and talk as a leader at TBI. It will be part of every leader's awareness, understanding, makeup, walk and mindset in the near future. These are maybe something like our Core Values or Principles, or some such terminology. What we call them is unimportant really. That we practice and model them is what's important....so begin soaking this up right now. From this day on, you can expect to get routine feedback and even on-the-spot corrections as we attempt to start changing our behaviors and what we *walk* around here. Some of you are likely still thinking of all this as some sort of 'program' but trust me that this is our new reality. Our vision for our company and our people, and will become yours." On the big screen, popped this:

Slide #12

TBI's VALUES and PRACTICES!

- 📖 **Consensus - Our way of doing business...**
- 📖 **What would Jesus do...?**
- 📖 **Maintaining, fixing & improving Relationships...**
- 📖 **Feedback routine and GOOD THING...**
- 📖 **Leaders growing people and teams...**
- 📖 **Leaders think Process & improve Systems...**
- 📖 **Everyone is my customer...**
- 📖 **Like those I work with / Fun place to work...**

"For now, let me just touch on each of these briefly," as he pointed to the screen.

Slide #13

CONSENSUS...

- **Leaders speak for their team, not themselves**
- **The issue goes down; solutions come up**
- **Means buy-in, support and 100% effort**
- **It is not MAJORITY RULES**
- **Everyone not in agreement, is against it**
- **Group dynamics and conflict will be present**

Slide #14

WHAT WOULD JESUS DO

- Our barometer
- Our source
- Treating others
- Teaching
- Judging others
- Trust
- Servant Leadership...

???????

Slide #15

RELATIONSHIPS

- Job #1
- Every Individual / Every Dept
- When damaged – Fix it
- A Performance Accountability

'Communication issues are Actually Relationship issues"

Slide #16

FEEDBACK IS A GOOD THING

- Viewed as a negative activity
- Hasn't been done *well* in our past
- Routine creates comfort
- Prevents surprise and unfairness
- Makes individuals/teams better...

Slide #17

GROWING PEOPLE & TEAMS

- We are improving or our leader is just maintaining
- Creating the next leader (the next you)
- Keeping people moving in a better position
- Don't accept them staying where they are
- No changing, no growing...

Slide #18

EVERYTHING IS A PROCESS / SYSTEM

- Leaders facilitate process
- Teams understand and provide input on improving process
- Leaders identify and resolve bottlenecks
- Processes routinely improved upon or reviewed
- People - your most important process
- Today is about creating a PEOPLE-SYSTEM
- Leaders go first...

Slide #19

EVERYONE IS CUSTOMER

- Wherever you look - they are customers
- Internal customers
- How we treat customers / friends
- Treat our own better than customers
- Get to know your customers...

Slide #20

HAPPY & FUN PLACE TO BE

- People come to work when it is friendly
- People enjoy coming to work when people are smiling
- People come when relationships are good
- Leaders facilitate people liking each other
- Turnover GOOD = People are happy
- Unhappy people = Ineffective leadership
- Trust, Open-ness and Belonging...

📖 Sooooooo.....Your thoughts?

Booker emphasized some points as he allowed people to read through the slides, before continuing, "Now all that is very nice, I am sure you will agree. However it doesn't just happen because we heard it here! This is about our personal behavioral changing, not a talk, like I am doing with you here right now. This talk will become our walk and your walk here, I assure you!

It takes leaders and leadership, all of us right here, right now to become facilitators of all this. We must buy into the vision that we have just explored over the last couple of hours; and then subsequently see that vision as ours and finally begin executing to reach it.

We must equip ourselves with the tools that leaders need, and that is coming gang. We are going to be providing you plenty of resources, mentoring, training and coaching. YOUR boss will be the key player in this, along with others that may be asked to help in providing skill training, etc.

This re-creation or rebuilding of each of us as leaders happens when we first understand our role. This set of competencies will be your accountabilities. Defining these and developing them is an initial step which is beginning right now. This is in the works, and be assured you will be a part of their development over the next couple of months. In case it is not obvious, you will be part of it because we are going to start modeling the right way of doing things in everything we do…involving people. From this day on, we are accepting the challenge to ensure we practice REAL LEADERSHIP and make decisions, implement changes and find solutions by using everyone's input. The days of saying we *want your input* and that you are the most valuable resource and then *walking something different* are over. Every leader with his or her team from the CEO down to the frontline Supervisor with their teams will be part of a total communication process, called a chain of command. The days of sending people and their ideas to a Suggestion Box that we place on the walls are over. Those 'distrust boxes' which I like to call them, will be gone by Monday. Developing trust and open-ness with your immediate leader and those ideas flowing upward is where we are headed.

As I wrap up my portion and hand this over to your CEO to close out the day, let me give you some immediate actions to consider. Every one of you is a leader over a team right now right? OK, so after digesting this all a bit, here is just a suggestion for the rebuilding of your team on rock. This is only a suggestion for now, if you feel secure and comfortable enough to take this and begin running with it. I'm not going to go into any great detail, but maybe you will get the essence of some of this and well, anything you do in these regards can only be a good thing huh? Consider this, as some initial work in REBUILDING YOUR ROCK!"

A new visual displayed on the big screen:

Slide #21

REBUILDING YOUR ROCK!

1. Dialogue with your boss
2. Begin VISIONING talks with your team
3. Ask your team what they want in their leader (YOU)
4. Observe/recognize behaviors that don't fit
5. Begin individual discussions with team members
6. Keep coming back to the traits and qualities of what they want in a leader-YOU
7. Change YOU
8. Keep discussions with your boss alive
9. Ask peers for input - improving YOU
10. Accept their criticism and input as if it is a good thing (because it is)
11. Challenge the team in team meetings regarding their relationships with each other, old baggage, current conflicts
12. Ask for help...there will be many dynamics that come up, that will be very challenging

---

As Booker finished summarizing this very briefly, he remembered back a few hours ago regarding his thoughts about Jesus turning the few loaves/fish into food for the masses. He still felt a connection to how this paralleled in some way what we were beginning today. We would begin to have these 70 turning the ideas and productivity of a few into the productivity of many! We will achieve amazingly higher levels of ideas, solutions, quality and productivity for TBI. Real leadership would do this.

He decided to let it go for now. The morning was getting away from us he thought, and he wanted to get the CEO up here and back to his family as quickly as possible anyway. There would be plenty more times for stories, teaching and yes maybe even preaching. He had done enough preaching for this day. He thought how he couldn't wait to see the fruits of these efforts begin to pay off, as leaders, people, teams and TBI would begin to grow…..into a ROCK.

He looked to the back of the auditorium spying the CEO sipping on a cup of coffee, and hollered, "You ready for these guys?" The CEO gestured something with Booker realizing he should give them a little break first. "You guys go stretch your legs, your minds and we'll see you back in here in a few to talk to the boss……our leader. I mean my leader; you know what I mean right?"

📖 While they take a break, are you applying all this, to your leadership role?

CEO TAKES THE STAGE – WRAPPING UP!

Mr. Gregg was on the stage walking around the podium, as people piled back in, ready to hear the BIG GUY. He always spoke in pretty quiet tones, making people really struggle to hear him at times. People respected him hugely and not just his title, so when he spoke, people really did want to listen and did. Hmmm?!?

He initially spoke of the vast importance of everything just shared at every level by every leader with every team. "I want you to clearly understand something about this day and going forward. We, as the leaders need to realize we are always modeling. Realizing this, I want you to know that what we did this morning will be rare, because in some ways it violates my own thinking - about talking to other people's folks."

He waited a moment, knowing that would cause a bit of confusion and allowing them all to ponder it. He jumped back in, "Let me explain what I just said. This is huge, so make sure you get this, digest it, talk to your boss about it, talk to your team about it, etc, later on – first chance. I am the leader at the top of TBI, but I am not really YOUR LEADER, I lead only eight people in this organization, my team. As a matter of fact, why don't you stand up if you are a member of my team? The eight stood, who were interspersed among the crowd. This they had actually planned, wanting to be strategically covering the entire audience to be able to pick up on comments, hear ideas, suggestions, concerns and maybe even clarify some things here and there.

"Thanks" he said, as the seven sat down and he continued, "that's the team that I am accountable to, and serve as their leader. Sure I am responsible for the entire organization and its results, but specific to leadership, that is my team. All the stuff you just heard Booker share this morning is for me to do with *my* team. You and I and everyone in this room, are going to become accountable for this stuff with our teams.

Booker and I jokingly call it 'stuff', since we are both anal about not liking titles, labels, programs, etc. We'll clean up the terminology with your help later - the competencies, principles, values, vision, and all that gobbledygook.

For now, just understand that this is all about behavioral changes we are going to begin focusing on; from top to bottom with our management and supervisors. That includes me and the eight members of my team. All means all. Every one of us will learn this stuff and much more as we take this organization to another level, maybe a *much* higher level my friends. We are indeed REBUILDING ON ROCK this time.

Slide #22

INVOLVEMENT = COMMITMENT

...we do this altogether...

I hope you have truly listened, thought about, digested and are considering how to internalize all this covered today. Our managing and maintaining days are done, or will be very soon. What will take its place is a whole organization with a bunch of teams and TEAMership. We will be 1000 people all about Relationships, Involving others, Growing people, Building teams, etc. Let me wrap this all up with this quote, which I know you have already seen this morning", as he pointed to the big screen. "Booker brought this to us, as you all know he uses it all the time. It has meaning that will become deep within TBI soon.

> **Slide #2 (again)**
>
> # "PEOPLE DON'T CARE HOW MUCH YOU KNOW UNTIL THEY FIRST KNOW HOW MUCH YOU CARE"
>
> *...as leaders, we need those people we serve, To think of us this way...*

This in some way will become the fiber of our existence around here, along with the principles Booker covered with you this morning. It will be part of every leader and eventually every employee here at TBI – our culture. Let me assure you that although I know some of you are viewing this as just warm n fuzzy, touchy feely stuff...it is much more than that. Let me go a step further and say to you, every leader sitting here, that if this is not you or something you don't prescribe to, you might want to be looking for other opportunities. We are all about keeping every one of you, and equipping you with the tools to succeed. Also know that we will have the right people on this rock with us!

If each of us doesn't care about those we lead, we don't belong in our leadership roles, bottom line. This is about a process of changing behaviors and thinking here at TBI, and growing people. That means growing you and your leadership. Guess who will do that teaching? It will be *your* boss, your leader who will become an effective coach, teacher, servant and facilitator. It will take a while, but in a year or two, we will be there.

You have, through the years, heard words like 'this time it will be different'. I get your skepticism, but will also expect that skepticism to go away quickly. We need your acceptance of the vision, understanding, attitude, open-ness of all this *to happen quickly*.

I will leave you with this – something I have come to call the Insanity Challenge. Insanity is defined, as we have all heard in various forms, as 'doing the same thing over and over and over again…and expecting different results'. One huge key to everything we will be doing will be about building relationships. Here's your first challenge. Get rid of a bit of insanity in your life by going and fixing a relationship of yours. Every one of us has at least one bad or ineffective relationship around here. This doesn't even necessarily mean it is bad in terms of a conflict, but it could be your worst relationship with someone here because he/she is new and you just haven't gotten to know them yet. Make sense? Bad relationships mean bad teamwork. So look around the room here, among your own team-members; go find that worst relationship, and whether they want to play, you make it happen, fix it. Now you might be sitting there thinking that maybe 'I can't do it by myself'. Let me offer this answer to that thinking", as he pointed to the projector screen, nodding for the slide to be shown….

> Slide #23
>
> ## *The Insanity of Unresolved Conflict*
>
> **If you cannot do this with your team-members/peers, how can we expect you to lead folks and help facilitate the fixing of relationships between members of YOUR team?**
>
> **This is a critical skill for a leader in the building of a real team? Think about that.**
>
> **If you cannot fix your own, can you or *will you* fix those you are responsible for...?"**
>
> ## *A SKILL OF THE 'NEW TBI LEADER'!*

Apply it to teams; the team you lead, the team you are a part of and other teams around you. You see bad relationships and conflicts here and there huh? Here is the deal. How insane is it for you or for anyone, to work all day long with ol' Doris, who you don't like, don't communicate with and tell others about? You wait for the day to get over with... It's like that GROUNDHOG DAY movie, the next day starts the same, Doris is there again, and that bad relationship. This goes on day after day after day after day after day........again like the movie huh? Is this insanity or what? And haven't all of us been there, done that or maybe are even doing that right now?

Remember the principle Booker described to you about creating a HAPPY and FUN environment. This cannot be the case when we are in one of these 'insanity conflicts', now can it? Annnnnnd if you are allowing that to go on within your team, then YOU are not leading according to our principles are you?

> 📖 Any thoughts what this INSANITY thing is all about? Have any in your life right now? Or those you lead?

And here's the kicker – while I am challenging you now in a light-hearted way to go fix that worst relationship; soon you will be accountable for it! Yes, accountable for strong relationships...let me assure you that *will* be one of our Competencies. This is about relationships with others on our level, our team-members, other department heads, internal customers, etc. You will be accountable to facilitate relationships getting better within your team. Before I leave this insanity thing, think about the positive impact on anytime, anywhere if every individual on the team was to fix the worst relationship? Ponder that for a moment.

Oh oh oh, one more *last thing* before we end this for today; and you will receive clarification on this over the coming weeks. We are putting all operational changes and implementations on somewhat of the back burner over the next year or so. You will receive more specific guidance and clarity regarding this. Just know that our top priority around here will be addressing our most important system & process – our PEOPLE SYSTEM! Fixing leaders and leadership is at the top of that priority, and that's us! Our Lean initiative will go on, but the true success of LEAN depends on the involvement of all people within an organization and the development of leaders at all levels, right?

I know there are tons of things on your mind and even specific questions, but because we made a commitment to be out of here by noon, and its 12:04 by my watch, let's adjourn. I am hanging around to eat lunch, talk with you all, as will the other members of MY TEAM! Let's go have lunch and then let's go fix relationships and start really leading people. As we close, please do me a favor, bow your head, and close your eyes, listen and think. Maybe even say a prayer – we will need lots of prayers as we go forward for sure.

After a moment, he concluded with, "Doc left this for us also to share with you as we finish today…"

Slide #24

Lord, I thank you for the wisdom to live an honorable life this day.
I will give you glory in all that I do and think.

I make my ways and my actions become in line
with what you would have me to be

Thank you for changing me Lord.

Thank you for helping me understand that although
I may not have been what I could have been yesterday, I know that
This Day, in the name of Jesus,
I am a new person in you.
I claim a new life in you and I am honest in all I say and do

I walk like you, I talk like you, and I am alive for you
I keep your commands and
I live each day full of integrity just like you would have me to.

I am strong in this life I live for you Lord,
and I thank you for the wisdom, the understanding, and
the desire to live an honorable life this day.

Amen

📖 Anything on your mind?

Part III

Applying all this to
YOUR WORLD!?!

Likely most of those reading this are leaders themselves, although all may not be sitting at the top of a large organization. This part of our work is intended to provide some connectivity between this book's content and worlds other than the mid to large size company depicted in our story here. Although we are sure you have seen plenty to connect with already, we wanted to provide some brief thoughts and additional thinking specific to OTHER WORLDS - communities, small businesses, stand-alone offices, churches, schools as well as just a brief discussion for any manager anywhere!

The following is presented to further stimulate your thinking; or offer some challenges and solutions to REBUILDING on ROCK, for YOUR WORLD.

1. Maybe you are a mid-level manager/supervisor in an organization (where you can't immediately fix the whole place,

but would like to apply all <u>this to your own team, office group or department)!</u>

First off, you must recognize that your own boss may be an issue; how we are led definitely can impact how *we* lead. If he/she is not a leader in the ways we have discussed here, you will have to use some finesse in doing a fair amount of what I call 'upward coaching'. You will need to think through most everything you do and consider how your boss might deal with your rebuilding. It will take much tactful and thoughtful communicating for sure.

Now for those *you* lead, this will take a huge commitment and plenty of persistence to deal with all the old baggage, behaviors and 'ways'. You may have caused them or a previous manager(s), but regardless you are their leader now and have to realize how leaders are viewed. It is important to understand that they may have dealt with nothing but ineffective leadership and you are just the next one! One recommendation to get the ball rolling, other than just lots of talk about all this routinely, is for you to open yourself up. Here's one way, briefly described: Have a brainstorming session with the team, asking what they want in a leader/you? You must now sincerely and clearly state to them that this list is what you want their help in improving – the traits, qualities and behaviors they just described to you (about you)! For you to change behavior you need reinforcement; the ones you lead are your best helpers in this regard. That seems awkward and strange, but also obviously true, isn't it? Give them permission and NEVER abuse this permission or request…….to catch you when you are not behaving well according to these traits. Even say THANKS when they do catch you. You will likely have to do some mentoring *after the fact* with some - regarding 'tact'. As they may not always deliver their thinking in nice way, just remember that all this is new to them as well. Everyone will grow if you are committed and persist. As we mentioned earlier, we must be about that awesome quote: FAILURE IS NOT AN OPTION.

In continuing on, you will have to *frequently* review these traits and let them evaluate you based on these. Likely you need to create a form with these and maybe even throw them up on a PowerPoint (or some AV) to create a long-term focus on these qualities, traits and behaviors. As you talk about/to these traits each time, you are teaching (don't forget this), and holding some very valuable discussion with the team. You see - all of these traits and behaviors really apply to all of us in any relationship (leader, follower, co-worker, and employee). Learning is going to be happening in all directions, with all, as you focus on improving you!

> 📖 You might want to THINK on this for a moment!

Again, you must go FIRST and keep the focus on 'working on you'. This process is really never ending, but with persistence after a few months, you will realize some major headway. You will *know* when you can let up a bit and even start turning things around and begin a full-fledged effort on evaluating them based on a similar process. Turning the direction to focusing on 'them' can be much the same deal in many ways. Brainstorm what we should expect out of team-members, employees, workers, each other, etc. You will see that this list is very similar to the one they are evaluating you on.... Now however, you can tweak it and make it an evaluation/assessment form and process for beginning formal routine (at least monthly) sessions with individuals and the team focusing on our rebuilding effort...LEADERSHIP, RELATIONSHIPS and TEAMERSHIP!

2. <u>Maybe you are a Small Business Owner (or Independent Office setting)!</u>

You are the boss with no one over you; well except the customers themselves....which is for another topic/another day. Regarding those you lead, whether that is two or fifteen, the process described above is totally pertinent to your world. And before you consider NOT doing any of this, consider this: TBI, our company in the story here, began as a small business. Do you realize how difficult it will be to fix this stuff and REBUILD later if you wait? Trust me - a lack of focus on all this now will very likely *do you in* down the road. We have all heard the outrageous statistics of how small businesses fail? Well, trust me, this is one of those reasons right here! BUILD on ROCK right now from the beginning and never lose focus of developing your people system as you grow. Also believe this; you WILL GROW if you focus on these dynamics!

3. Maybe you are the Superintendent or Principal <u>over a school or a school system!</u>

This book overall along with the discussion just above, will likely be all you need. Your biggest challenges will likely be staying the course, commitment and persistence of the ROCK-stuff. Additionally you will need to ensure you clearly have the chain of command clarified and people know who their leader is – this gets blurred in school settings frequently. Some of that blurring comes from counselors, board members, vice-principals, secretaries, etc. The school team (of administrators, board members and teachers) that executes strong relationships, a clear chain of command understanding; and unity is one that will succeed. It should be very obvious to students, parents and community – that you are a LEADERSHIP TEAM, or not.

4. <u>Maybe you are a Church Senior Pastor!</u>

If this is you, you know that you have some of the more unique leadership challenges in this world! Briefly, I will just mention a few thoughts for your consideration. First of all, realize that in terms of Leadership Qualities and Traits...and Behaviors, you are no different than all we have just described in this book. You do not just possess these leader qualities naturally and your church didn't really check them out upon bringing you on board. Again, the lack of these types of traits and behaviors is typically discovered after the fact. Hopefully you will realize these shortcomings and take some self-improvement actions, before they realize them. If you are a great preacher, have a close personal relationship with our Savior and know the bible inside and out – you still need LEADERSHIP. Power can be a tricky issue for the Pastor, just as it can be for any leader or manager anywhere. If you believe you have all the answers and have the right/power to dictate how things will be, well the Leadership Dilemma is alive! I know this all can get touchy here, but there is also the issue of the leader believing he has a *connection* to the way things should be (God speaking to you directly). While this may be the reality, people won't just always naturally follow this way of leading. Creating consensus is definitely something pastors need a great understanding of, and again, all this doesn't come naturally. Enough for now.

5. Maybe you are the Mayor or City <u>Administrator, for a community!</u>

Everything here in this book is clearly applicable to your world, but at least two other major challenges may exist: 1) just as within the church setting, much of what needs to happen and get done comes from volunteers – you know this. However, with solid RELATIONSHIPS, LEADERSHIP and TEAMERSHIP happening, this doesn't need to be a big deal/difference. People *will* follow *real* leadership! 2) Another dynamic that needs addressing and receiving focus is diversity and cliques. Tons of dynamics may be present challenging the functioning of the community – groups/cliques that may have even begun when people were in school! These have carried through and now they are adults - but still the territories persist. Additionally, new people move in, and without some introductory process to people in the community, these 'outsiders' frequently just fall into the trap and clique(s) they stumble into... OR they become disenchanted at how difficult it is to 'break in' to the community. The Leadership Dilemma is maybe more of an issue here than any other leadership situation. The individual at the top (mayor, etc) may not only be missing critical leadership skills but also may possess no real understanding of how the city/community works. Ruh Roh! ☺☹ Very often, this position is held because of some political dynamic; he/she was a good person that was popular, some group got them voted in, nobody else wanted it, etc. Regardless, it is the same old challenge, the leader not possessing the leadership *stuff*. Finally, a major obstacle is the lack of a leadership TEAM. Due to things not being done in a systematic way (over years and even decades), there is no real leadership chain of command present. There are committees, groups, the council, clubs, cliques, the chamber maybe, etc. Again, we are not speaking of 'bad people', but 'bad practices'. All of these do not always work smoothly together, under a clearly communicated, accepted and understood chain of command. You are thinking, 'no kidding, huh?'

"Maybe it is a good time to mention Again, that NONE of this is about 'Bad people'. This is about understanding and becoming aware of our leadership challenge! If we add in the possibility that it is about a bad person,

...we have a huge RUH ROH"

CONCLUSION

If you are a leader, I hope you are at least more aware of what is challenging you, your team, organization, etc. As your mentor and servant, I will be available anytime you would like to discuss, argue or brainstorm any of these dynamics. I am obviously happy to help with your world! That's a totally sincere invitation for you to contact me if you would like to explore any of this further.

This book and my previous work are here to make organizations and individuals realize how much of a void we have when it comes to understanding and developing leaders. The first story (first book) 'Teaching Fishing' was offered as an awareness – an initial step to grow, understand and learn about individual and organizational challenges. This second book hopefully serves to provide some answers as you evolve and transform yourself and others.

YOUR AUTHOR & STORY-TELLER

Doug Booker

As President and Founder of Booker Training Associates, Doug is a Professional Facilitator, Management Coach, Teacher, Author and Organizational Developer. In 1992, following a successful military career, Doug accepted an early retirement/buy-out from the Army Infantry, achieving the rank of Major.

A strong believer in the need for continued learning; he has attended numerous professional development courses & schools and earned a Masters in Management. He also completed an Executive MBA program, as well as a Lean Business & Manufacturing certification. He considers his strengths to be his understanding of leadership, adult learning, challenging human relations, organizational behavior, developing critical thinking, along with a natural sense of humor. He possesses a unique ability to relate to people, facilitate change and challenge leader's thinking!

He provides honest consultation and advice to clients along with Executive Leadership Coaching. He also writes and distributes a series of leadership articles and briefs (Leadership Moments) along with authoring two books, the third 'on the way'.

Doug regards his Savior, Jesus Christ; his wife Sydney, two children (Lesa/JD) and family…along with *helping people* as the best aspects of his life. His recognition as the U.S. Army's Officer Leadership Developer of the Year in 1990 was the result of one of the most rewarding positions of his military career; as an ROTC Mentor and Faculty member at Kansas State University. Along with growing from a great learning experience, Doug was recognized by the Secretary of Defense in Washington D.C., after being selected as the sole Army designee from over 350 nominees nationwide.

He continues his love of learning serving as a faculty member with three universities. For the last seven years he has taught business management courses at the Graduate levels. He resides outside the Kansas City area (Lexington, MO) with his wife, assisting communities and churches in leadership as well.

Co-authors

Derek Kenner, Ph.D.

Over the past 36 years Derek Kenner, Ph.D. has operated in a number of educational, sales-related and training roles. During that time his primary goal has been to change people's lives for the better. The focus of his work included management consulting, curriculum development, instruction and training, and leadership development; to both non-profit and for-profit corporations.

Currently, Dr. Kenner serves as a Lead Performance Consultant at a global Fortune 150 company in the Midwest where he is responsible for organizational development, performance consultation, talent development, training, and coaching for sales, marketing, staffing, and professional employees.

Dr. Kenner is also an author and consultant on many faith- based endeavors. In addition, he serves as the founder and Managing Director of The Kenner Group, an organizational development and performance / management consulting firm founded in 1997. He was a founding partner and President of Union Heritage Capital Management, Inc., an investment banking firm in Detroit, Michigan and a founding partner and Managing Director of SBK Brooks Investment, Inc., an affiliated institutional brokerage firm headquartered in Cleveland, Ohio. He also was a founding member and President of KB & A, Inc., a firm providing financial consulting services to major municipalities and corporations.

Dr. Kenner holds a Ph.D. in Urban Education and a M.S. in Curriculum and Instruction from the University of Wisconsin – Milwaukee. He has a B.S. in Liberal Arts Studies and Psychology from Carroll College in Waukesha, Wisconsin. He served as a Kellogg National Fellow (Group 14), from September 1, 1994 through August 31, 1997. He currently is the Chairman of the Faith Partnership Network, Inc. in Milwaukee and serves as the Director of Operations at Walking in the Spirit Ministries in West Allis, Wisconsin.

Dr. Kenner lives in Milwaukee, Wisconsin with his wife Donna and is a proud and loving father and grandfather.

Derekkenner1@gmail.com

…find Derek on Facebook (Drambert Publishing) & Linked In

Mark Broadway

Originally from Jonesboro, Arkansas, Mark learned early in life from strong Christian parents that life's greatest priorities are God, family and work, always in that order. He attended Arkansas State University graduating with a BS degree in Physics. After being accepted by some prestigious schools for Graduate Studies, he was also accepted into the Manufacturing Management Program at General Electric (GE). Mark received an offer to join GE, beginning a professional career immediately upon graduation from ASU, choosing GE over continuing his education.

Since these early days with GE, he has now spent 30+ years working in manufacturing plants, 20+ of those years as a Plant Manager or Senior Business Leader. Experience has taught him that people are the greatest asset of any business, but; people cannot reach their true potential without learning to fish, and it is the leader's responsibility to teach them to do so. Relationships form foundations for success, in all areas of life, but leadership is the cornerstone for building the future.

Mark currently resides in Elkins, Arkansas, near Fayetteville, with his wife Becky and his two grandchildren, Blayne and Autumn. Professionally, he is currently the Vice President of Quality Assurance for Pace Industries, the largest non-automotive aluminum die casting company in North America. In his spare time Mark enjoys fishing, hunting and the great outdoors with his family. Mark and Doug met over 16 years ago. Doug provided management and leadership development training for Mark on several occasions, teaching many of those that Mark worked with *how to fish* while forming a close personal friendship.

markbroadway@earthlink.net

📖 *...any last ideas, plans, actions or intentions to capture here before we finish?*

Appendix 1: Presentation Slides

"PEOPLE DON'T CARE HOW MUCH YOU KNOW, UNTIL THEY FIRST KNOW HOW MUCH YOU CARE."

Credit given to John Maxwell

Another favorite sarcastic quote of mine, <u>about leaders and leadership</u>

"I'm not BOSSY, I just have better ideas..."

* Think about it *

The rain came down, the streams rose, and the winds blew and beat against that house;
Yet it did not fall, because it had its foundation on the rock.

- o micro-managing leaders vs leaders that involve and ask others their thoughts
- o
- o bottlenecks within teams in the form of conflicts
- o baggage, etc between folks
- o people jumping the chain of command & skipping over others to get the answer they want
- o
- o people wanting to be right vs getting the right/best answer to problems
- o
- o people talking about others
- o territories, silos, agendas of individuals and departments

! LEADER*ship*

! TEAMER*ship*

! RELATION*ship*

You <u>can't not</u>
'LEAD BY EXAMPLE'!
...think about it...

I would rather <u>see</u> a sermon
Than <u>hear</u> one any day...
I'd rather you would walk with me,
Than merely show the way...
The lectures you deliver
May be very wise and true,
But I think I'll get my lesson
By watching what you do...
Because I might misunderstand you,
And all the high advice you give,
But there's no misunderstanding
How you act and how you live

We are <u>ALWAYS</u>...
'LEADING BY EXAMPLE'
...think about it...!

(Anonymous author)

TBI's VALUES and PRACTICES!

- Consensus - Our way of doing business...
- What would Jesus do...?
- Maintaining, fixing & improving Relationships...
- Feedback routine and GOOD THING...
- Leaders growing people and teams...
- Leaders think Process & Facilitate improve Systems...
- Everyone is my customer...
- Like those I work with / Fun place to work...

CONSENSUS...

- Leaders speak for their team, not themselves
- The issue goes down; solutions come up
- Means buy-in, support and 100% effort
- It is not MAJORITY RULES
- Everyone not in agreement, is against it
- Group dynamics and conflict will be present

LEADERSHIP PERFORMANCE COMPETENCIES
(For use in mentoring, hiring, coaching, evaluation, feedback, performance, firing, training, promotion, etc)

BUSINESS KNOWLEDGE (education, self-development, development of others, follower's knowledge, operational/technical...

COMMUNICATION SKILLS (counseling, listening, people informed, written/oral, expectations, presentation & facilitation skills, team communications, internal customers...

PROBLEM SOLVING / DECISION MAKING (judgment, conflict resolution, use of consensus, reasoning, creative...

SENSITIVITY (caring, respect, fairness, safety of people, understanding, supporting, loyalty, compassion, organizational support, approachable...

CHANGE FACILITATION (people empowered, open to other ideas, OK being wrong, open-minded, adaptive, flexibility, systems/process thinking, continuous improvement...

MOTIVATION (teaching, inspiring, charisma, growing people and teams, delegation, influence, turnover, involves people...

PRODUCTIVITY/RESULTS (making it happen, endurance, mission accomplishment, attainment of goals...

PLANNING and ORGANIZING (time management, plans, goals, dependability/reliability, controlling...

PROFESSIONALISM (appearance, accountable, presence, followership, standards, people skills, team-player, relationships, role model, tact...

ETHICS and VALUES (work ethic, honest, values, culture, integrity, admits mistakes...

WHAT WOULD JESUS DO

- Our barometer
- Our source
- Treating others
- Teaching
- Judging others
- Trust
- Servant Leadership...

RELATIONSHIPS

- Job #1
- Every Individual / Every Dept.
- When damaged – Fix it
- A Performance Accountability

'Communication issues are Actually Relationship issues"

FEEDBACK IS A GOOD THING

- Viewed as a negative activity
- Hasn't been done *well* in our past
- Routine creates comfort
- Prevents surprise and unfairness
- Makes individuals/teams better...

GROWING PEOPLE & TEAMS

- We are improving or our leader is just maintaining
- Creating the next leader (the next you)
- Keeping people moving in a better position
- Don't accept them staying where they are
- No changing, no growing...

EVERYTHING IS A PROCESS / SYSTEM

- Leaders facilitate process
- Teams understand and provide input on improving process
- Leaders identify and resolve bottlenecks
- Processes routinely improved upon or reviewed
- People - your most important process
- Today is about creating a PEOPLE-SYSTEM
- Leaders go first...

EVERYONE IS CUSTOMER

- Wherever you look - they are customers
- Internal customers
- How we treat customers / friends
- Treat our own better than customers
- Get to know your customers...

HAPPY & FUN PLACE TO BE

- People come to work when it is friendly
- People enjoy coming to work when people are smiling
- People come when relationships are good
- Leaders facilitate people liking each other
- Turnover GOOD = People are happy
- Unhappy people = Ineffective leadership
- Trust, Open-ness and Belonging...

INVOLVEMENT = COMMITMENT

...we do this altogether...

The Insanity of Unresolved Conflict

If you cannot do this, how can we expect you to lead folks and help facilitate the fixing of relationships between members of YOUR team?

This is a critical skill for a leader in the building of a real team? Think about that.

If you cannot fix your own, can you or *will you* fix those you are responsible for...?"

A SKILL OF THE 'NEW TBI LEADER'!

REBUILDING on ROCK

1. Dialogue with your boss
2. Begin VISIONING talks with your team
3. Ask your team what they want in their leader (YOU)
4. Observe/recognize behaviors that don't fit
5. Begin individual discussions with team members
6. Keep coming back to the traits and qualities of what they want in YOU
7. Change YOU
8. Keep discussions with your boss alive
9. Ask peers for input - improving YOU
10. Accept their criticism and input as if it is a good thing (because it is)
11. Challenge the team in team meetings regarding their relationships with each other, old baggage, and current conflicts
12. Ask for help...many dynamics will come up, that will be very challenging!

Acknowledgement Statement
INFO, REFERENCES and MATERIALS

I have spent nearly twenty years in training, consulting, coaching and providing resources to organizations. During this time, I have learned and grown in my own thinking; and incorporated other's thinking into my own.

I neither claim that all of this was 'thought up' on my own, nor that it is all my original thoughts. Rather I am acknowledging that I have undoubtedly learned, digested and borrowed thoughts (intentionally and unintentionally). Again, I have attempted to take all of what I have captured and shared it all with you here, within my first two books.

I absolutely have not intended to borrow, steal or plagiarize from others without giving credit. If I have accidentally done so, I sincerely apologize. Let me know and I will gladly recognize any credit that should be given within my next book.

Sincerely, Doug Booker

Appendix 2: Scriptures

The following is intended to be a brief listing of scriptures that tie to our lessons here of Leadership, Relationships, Learning, Teaching and Growing.

2 Chronicles 1:10 (NI) "Give me **wisdom** and knowledge, that I may **lead** this people, for who is able to govern this great people of yours?"

1 Corinthians
   8:1 (NI) "…We know that we all possess knowledge. **Knowledge puffs up, but love builds up.** The man who thinks he knows something does not yet know as he ought to know…"

   10: 3-4 (NI) "They all ate the same spiritual food and drank the same spiritual drink; for they drank from the spiritual rock that accompanied them, and that rock was **Christ**."

Daniel 2:34 (NI) "While you were watching, **a rock was cut out, but not by human hands**…"

Deuteronomy
   4:6 (NI) "Observe them carefully, for this will show your **wisdom** and understanding to the nations, who will hear about all these decrees and say, 'Surely this **great nation** is a wise and understanding people'…"

   32:4 (NI) "He is the Rock, his works are perfect, and all his ways are just."

Isaiah
   26:4 (NI) "**Trust** in the Lord forever, for the Lord, the Lord is the Rock eternal"

51:1 (NI) "Listen to me, you who pursue righteousness and who seek the Lord; **look to the rock** from which you were cut and to the quarry from which you were hewn…"

Job 34:2 (NI) "Hear my words, you wise men; listen to me, you men of **learning**"

1 Kings 4:29 (NI) "God gave Solomon **wisdom** and very great insight, and a breadth of understanding as measureless as the sand on the seashore."

10:8 (NI) "How happy your men must be! How happy your officials, who continually stand before you and hear your **wisdom**!"

Mark
1:22 (NI) "The **people** were amazed at his **teaching**, because he taught them as one who had authority, not as the teachers of the law."

Matthew
10:24 (NI) "A student is not above his teacher, nor a servant above his master."

16:18 (NI) "And I tell you that you are Peter, and **on this rock I will build my church**..."

9:33 (NI) "See I lay in Zion a stone that causes men to stumble and a rock that makes them fall, and the one who trusts in Him will never be put to shame."

Philippians 4:9 (NI) "Whatever you have learned or received or heard from me, or seen in me-put it into practice." And the **God of peace** will be with you."

Proverbs
1:5 (KJ) "A wise [man] will hear, and will increase learning; and a man of understanding shall attain unto wise counsels"

3:13 (KJ) "**Happy [is] the man [that] fended wisdom**, and the man [that] getteth understanding".

Psalms 90:15 (NI) "Make us glad for as many days as you have afflicted us, for as many years as we have seen trouble"

90:17 (NI) "May the favor of the Lord our God rest upon us; establish the work or our hands for us…"

2 Peter 3:15 (NI) "Bear in mind that our Lord's **patience** means salvation, just as our dear brother Paul also wrote you with the **wisdom** that God gave him."

2 Samuel 22:2 (NI) "The Lord is my rock, my fortress and my deliverer; my God is my rock, in whom I take refuge…"

Ultimately this book
And everything
I do in this awesome world and life,
Is dedicated to
My Savior, Jesus Christ.

Thank you, Lord
For all my blessings, and
Bless leaders and
Those they lead, everywhere.

May this be pleasing to you?
And according to your Will.
Please allow for all who read to learn and
Be open to change
In their hearts and minds.

If you enjoyed and found this second book to be a 'good thing', please let us know! Maybe you know others who might find it useful - or maybe you know someone that 'should' read it! Let us know and we will be happy to contact them. ☺

www.bookertraining.com
doug@bookertraining.com
913.232.0244

"Never stop Learning ...
Never stop Growing"

www.ingramcontent.com/pod-product-compliance
Lightning Source LLC
Chambersburg PA
CBHW051808170526
45167CB00005B/1927